THE INK IS DRY

THE INK IS DRY

God's Distinctive Word on Marriage, Family, and Sexual Responsibility

RUBEL SHELLY

college press
Joplin, Missouri

**The Ink Is Dry: God's Distinctive Word on
Marriage, Family, and Sexual Responsibility**

Copyright 2023

Rubel Shelly

ISBN: 978-0-89900-104-3 (paperback)
ISBN: 978-0-89900-105-0 (hardback)
ISBN: 978-0-89900-106-7 (eBook)

On the web at www.collegepress.com

All Scripture quotations, unless otherwise indicated, are taken from the Holy Bible, New International Version®, NIV®. Copyright ©1973, 1978, 1984, 2011 by Biblica, Inc.™ Used by permission of Zondervan. All rights reserved worldwide. www.zondervan.com. The "NIV" and "New International Version" are trademarks registered in the United States Patent and Trademark Office by Biblica, Inc.™

If you don't need this book, someone you love does! The cultural confusion around gender has traumatized teens and their parents. Shelly provides a scriptural guide through the malaise that can help soothe beleaguered souls with biblical truths.

—MARK MOORE
Teaching Pastor, Christ's Church of the Valley
Phoenix, Arizona

In *The Ink is Dry*, Rubel Shelly underscores timeless truths about marriage, family, and sexual responsibility in a grace-filled way. His intended audience is not "out there" somewhere – "for what business is it of mine to judge those outside the church?" He is speaking to the Body of Christ grappling with these issues, feeling the pull of a hyper-sexualized culture that blesses behaviors Scripture does not endorse. Truth without grace isn't the whole truth. But grace without truth isn't true grace. This book is full of both grace and truth.

—MONTE COX
Dean, College of Bible and Ministry
Harding University

This may well be the best short book setting forth the classic Christian view of same-sex attraction and gay marriage. It is biblically robust, well informed by recent historical scholarship, and deeply compassionate – written without a trace of rancor and without a political agenda. It will call you, wherever you are in your present understanding, to embrace the Judeo-Christian tradition's over three-millennia-old commitment to God's design for sex and marriage.

—LEONARD ALLEN,
author of *Poured Out: The Spirit of God Empowering the Mission of God*

Are we autonomous animals whose sole end is pleasure or created images of God whose end is to become like God in true love and holiness? The Scriptures clearly affirm the latter, while some contemporary interpreters treat the Scriptures as if they were written in erasable ink or even in pencil. For Rubel Shelly, however, *The Ink Is Dry*. Shelly guides us in a study of the most significant texts in the Old and New Testaments that deal with same-sex sexual behavior. He sets these passages in their historical contexts and deals with the clever, and often deceptive, maneuvers of interpreters who dispute their commonsense meanings. I especially appreciate the way Shelly places passages in the context of God's beautiful creational design for marriage between man and woman. I highly recommend *The Ink is Dry* to preachers, elders, college students, youth leaders, teachers, counselors, and anyone else concerned about the moral challenges facing the church today. Readers will find it useful for group and individual study.

—RON HIGHFIELD
Professor of Religion
Pepperdine University

Local churches can ask hard questions; especially as it relates to matters of sexuality, the body, and God's purpose for our lives. Rubel's book, *The Ink is Dry,* provides a clear framework for understanding the historic and traditional position of "accepting but not affirming." He is gracious, while also standing on the conviction that we need to have intimate conversations about what we do with our desires and how we understand our place before Creator God.

—JOSH GRAVES
author of *The Simple Secret*

Rubel Shelly has invited us into a safe discussion in a very controversial subject that most churches cannot talk about. He reminds of us of God's call to authentic biblical sexuality for all His people. As you turn the pages, you will be blessed with current research, historical insights, and deep theological discernment.

—ROBERT OGLESBY
Director, Center for Youth and Family Ministry
Abilene Christian University

The Ink Is Dry is a handy resource for parents and youth leaders who are trying to provide guidance to children struggling with gender dysphoria issues. This helpful book also provides ready reference material for teachers searching for ways to communicate a positive message on what the Bible says about sexual behavior.

—BOB RUSSELL
Retired Sr. Minister,
Southeast Christian Church
Louisville, Kentuckhy

Designed for personal study, small groups, and/or church classes, Rubel Shelly addresses the core questions surrounding same-sex behavior. With pastoral sensitivity and incisive probing, he walks us through the story of Scripture (including creation, Israel, Jesus, and Paul) within its cultural context to offer a credible case for the historic Christian ethic: "God blesses the union of one male to one female in a covenant commitment that provides the context for procreation, nurture, and love for the original pair and any children who may be born to them." Its length and non-technical nature optimizes accessibility and practical use for all readers. Read it; it is worth your time!

—JOHN MARK HICKS
Professor of Theology
Lipscomb University

Rubel Shelly's second volume dealing with the LGBTQ+ conversation, *The Ink Is Dry*, offers a summary of his previous work but also serves two important functions. First, it provides an excellent introduction to the issues involved. Second, as a preliminary study, it can serve as an outline for anyone desiring the more in-depth study of the larger volume. The book is ideal for classroom study and will prove to be a valuable resource in that capacity. With crisp organization and engaging writing style, Shelly delivers a readable book for any age group.

—JERRY JONES
Leader of *Marriage Matters*

We live in days where a fluidity about sexual identity persists. Into this cultural questioning, Shelly rightly enters the conversation asking for careful consideration of what the Bible has to say on the issues. His focus is important and this book is a valuable read for anyone.

—MARK LANIER
Founder, *Lanier Law Firm*
Author, Attorney, Minister

The more I read of this book the more I loved it. Rubel Shelly's historical analysis overturns assertions that the Bible only addresses exploitative homosexual behavior because committed same-sex relationships did not exist until recent times. His sharp exegesis and discussion of Old Testament and New Testament texts may be the best I have seen on this topic. His analysis of the cultural trends that have brought us here are insightful and remind us that remaining rooted in a biblical worldview is crucial to being Christian. Best of all, he paints a beautiful, positive picture of God's vision for an alternative kingdom community where there is welcoming love and healing transformation. Our world is weary and hungry for a third way – a way that embraces both moral clarity and gracious love. Rubel reminds us to be God's faithful people for just such a time as this!

—JIMMY ADCOX
Southwest Church of Christ, Jonesboro, Arkansas

The Ink is Dry is a must read for any parent, pastor, teacher, or counselor searching for a well-researched historical and biblical context for understanding today's gender issues.

—MATTHEW SLEETH, MD
author of *Hope Always, 24/6,* and *Reforesting Faith*

TABLE OF CONTENTS

Foreword	7
1. Jesus Loves You, This I Know . . .	21
2. This Goes Back to Eden	43
3. A World in Rebellion	65
4. What the Old Testament Says	81
5. What the New Testament Says	107
6. Why Perspectives Have Changed	133
Afterword	161
Index of Scriptures	173
Index of Persons & Subjects	175
Acknowledgements	181

> *Haven't you read that at the beginning the Creator 'made them male and female'?*
>
> – Jesus of Nazareth

FOREWORD

If you are driving down the highway and see a red light blinking on your vehicle's instrument panel, you'd be wise to pay attention. Tire pressure, engine temperature, seat belt reminder, low fuel – some are more critical than others, but each warning light means something. When one flashes on your dashboard, it means that something isn't working the way it should. The same thing is true of warning signals we encounter in other settings.

We Have a Cultural Problem

The analytics of what is going on in American culture right now look very much like a series of flashing red lights. We are being warned of some basic malfunctions in the social engine that drives our culture. The signals are there for all to see. My personal fear is that we are shielding our eyes rather than taking action to address the problems. In some cases, people may be taking a hammer to their instrument panels (i.e., destroying the warning signals) rather than making an effort to fix what is broken.

Some polling numbers I have seen from the Gallup organization have Americans lamenting that the general moral climate in the country is anything but wholesome. Fully 50% rate the overall state of our moral values as "poor." Another 37% rate it "only fair," and a barely registering 1% say the state of our moral tenets is "excellent." (For comparison, on average since 2002, some 43% of U.S. adults have rated moral values in the U.S. as "poor" and 18% as "excellent" or "good.") Furthermore, 78% of the respondents in that same poll said they believe American morals are getting worse instead of better.[1]

What encourages me in that same report is that – when asked to state the most important issue driving them to their negative assessment – the people being polled said it was consideration for other persons. In other words, what Sunday School children once learned as the Golden Rule seems to have been abandoned by too many of us. However, when you add the 18% who said "consideration of others" to the second-highest item of concern – "racism/discrimination" at 8% – it turns out that one-quarter of the population is saying we need to learn how to love one another. We must put an end to the senseless divisiveness that has become standard fare in political campaigns, city council meetings, church business meetings, and family get-togethers.

As a nation, it would be a huge step forward in our collective moral life to learn to get along with one another. At an intellectual level, all of us know that what provides cable news ratings, hits on websites, podcast audiences, and election-day victories is the verbal equivalent of a street brawl. In the meanwhile, we continue to undermine the most basic of all human relationships. And that most basic relationship is not labor-management, contract law, partisan politics, capitalism and its alternatives, or even West versus East. As significant as each of these concerns may be to

---

[1] Megan Brenan and Nicole Willcoxon, "Record-High 50% of Americans Rate U.S. Moral Values as 'Poor'," *Gallup* (June 15, 2022), https://news.gallup.com/poll/393659/record-high-americans-rate-moral-values-poor.aspx.

our collective welfare, the most basic of all human relationships is the first one identified in the Bible – *personal relationships within marriage and family.*

In their analysis of America's moral climate, the Gallup researchers point to "a shift away from normative standards proscribing certain behaviors that arose through practice, tradition and religious teachings."[2]

> Americans have become significantly more open to things to which they were previously closed – ranging from cloning humans to polygamy – as well as broad questions about their views of moral values more generally. . . .
>
> Americans' views that each of the following is morally acceptable has increased significantly over the past two decades: sex between an unmarried man and woman, having a baby outside of marriage, sex between teenagers, and gay or lesbian relations. And while just 23% of Americans say that polygamy is morally acceptable, that's up from 7% in 2003. . . .
>
> In essence, Americans are becoming more accepting as far as non-traditional families and sexual behavior are concerned.[3]

"Ah, here we go!" someone says. "Another preacher rant about sex. Why can't you church people mind your own business and quit trying to tell the rest of us how to live? We can do quite well without your meddling, your judgmental attitudes, and your threats that the rest of us are going to Hell for daring to make personal decisions and live with our own choices. It's my body. It's my choice. It's none of *your* business to try to make me live by *your* rules."

I get it. I both understand and, for the most part, agree with that response. Please bear with me as I try to explain.

---

[2] Frank Newport, "Untangling Americans' Complex Views of Morality," *Gallup* (June 17, 2022), https://news.gallup.com/opinion/polling-matters/393782/untangling-americans-complex-views-morality.aspx.
[3] Ibid.

Focusing the Subject Matter

The overarching concern of this little book is *Christian ethics*. Ethical reasoning must proceed by means of sound principles which, in turn, will generate norms to guide behavior. In the case of Christian ethics, those principles derive from God's personal holiness and both model and demand what is moral for his worshippers. Thus the repeated command for both ancient Israel and then the church to be set apart from the defilement of sin: "Be holy, for I am holy" (Lev 11:44-45; 19:2; 20:7,26; 21:8; 1 Pet 1:16; cf. Ex 19:6; 1 Thess 4:7, etc.).

Since the moral insights and commandments in the Bible are rooted in God's inherent goodness and holy character, they cannot be other than they are. Because God is the same yesterday, today, and forever, the ethical demands that he gives through revelation cannot change from person to person, nation to nation, or generation to generation. Therefore, what the Bible says about the unjustified taking of a life, breaking one's covenant promise either to God or another human, loving as neighbors those who are not geographically or ethnically like us, or engaging in sex acts outside a male-female marriage commitment is true both for the moment when the words were first written and for all time. My way of saying that for the purposes of this book is to make the simple claim that *the ink is dry* on those topics. Specific to the issue of human sexuality, what the Bible says about premarital chastity, marital fidelity, same-sex behaviors, and related topics is fixed. It is not subject to revision by whim, romantic attraction, opinion polls, academic challenge, professional associations, courts, or legislatures.

Revisionists such as Matthew Vines, David Gushee, Adam Hamilton, and others root what they offer as an ethical-biblical case for same-sex marriage in an appeal to emotion rather than logical argument. They appeal to the statistical analysis of soft sciences such as sociology and psychology rather than the hard sciences of biology and genetics. Their methodology smacks of holding a desired conclusion and going in search of a case to support it. The very fact that their reinterpretation of the biblical data is couched – by their own admission – in terms of personal (Vines), family (Gushee), and friendship (Hamilton) considerations is significant. All of us tend to make gratuitous concessions for ourselves and to those we love. Not one of these affirming writers offers to make an affirmative case for same-sex behavior from Scripture. Their argument from the Bible is best summarized this way: *the Bible doesn't actually mean what Jews and Christians have understood it to say about same-sex activity for 3,000 years*. On their view, the ink of biblical revelation apparently was not indelible ink. It has either faded or was perhaps only nothing more than No. 2 lead pencil – subject to erasure and emendation. As you will learn in the pages that follow in this book, the revisionist case actually demands a move away from an orthodox view of biblical inspiration.

The specific issue of ethical concern in this volume is the contemporary controversy over same-sex behaviors. Let me be very clear about two issues from the beginning.

First, my concern is *not* to make a case for civil laws about same-sex marriage, civil unions, or domestic partnerships. A decision by the U.S. Supreme Court in 2003 essentially invalidated the so-called sodomy laws that were on the books in many states. Those laws had made it illegal for both opposite-sex and same-sex couples to participate in oral or anal sex or for anyone to have sex with an animal (i.e., bestiality).

Second, this study focuses exclusively on the historical and linguistic interpretation of biblical texts related to human sexuality in general and to same-sex intercourse in particular. Several revisionist scholars have offered *re*-interpretations of those texts of late. While they are not in agreement on what those texts *do* mean (i.e., cult prostitution, pederasty, genetic orientation, opposite-sex persons experimenting with same-sex activity, etc.), they share a commitment about what they *do not* mean (i.e., same-sex intercourse is not immoral for loving and committed partners, transgender choices should not be considered wrong, etc.).

To be more specific still, this study is not a political or cultural proposal. It is a Bible study that proposes to demonstrate that *Christian Scripture presents a view of marriage, family, and sexual responsibility that blesses the union of one male to one female in a covenant commitment that provides the context for procreation, nurture, and love for the original pair and any children who may be born to them.*

The summary of this thesis is found in the following biblical statement: "Marriage should be honored by all, and the marriage bed kept pure, for God will judge the adulterer and all the sexually immoral" (Heb 13:4). This is not offered as a "proof text" but is simply one biblical writer's summary of the issues to be addressed in this book.

The word "marriage" in this New Testament text refers to what that term has meant in its common usage for thousands of years. It affirms that this foundational structure to all human life and flourishing is not only blessed and protected by God but also "should be honored by all." To this positive declaration, the writer adds a negative warning to people who damage or undermine its crucial value. Specifically, an "adulterer" is someone who violates his or her own or another's marital covenant through either the married person having sexual contact with a third party or a third party who has sex with a married person.

It is basic to a marriage covenant that we still use language equivalent to these words from *The Book of Common Prayer*: "Will you forsake all others and be faithful to him/her as long as you both shall live?" The word translated "sexually immoral (person)" in the verse refers to anyone who has sexual intercourse in any setting other than within a marriage commitment with his or her covenanted partner. It is a broad term that includes consensual premarital sex, sex with or as a prostitute, forcible intercourse (i.e., rape), incest – in all these cases, whether opposite-sex or same-sex in nature – or even bestiality.

Hebrews 13:4, with its dual blessing and warning, is not a proposal its original writer made to the Roman Emperor as a replacement statute for the empire's very lax moral standards. The Romans valued traditional marriage, yet their laws and cultural norms allowed husbands to have near-unlimited sexual freedom but required wives to be exclusive to their husbands as sexual partners. Men visited brothels without shame. Wealthy Roman males exploited their slaves – both female and male – for sexual favors with immunity from censure. There were illicit affairs by married persons. There were long-term committed relationships between two male partners or two female partners – sometimes even termed "marriages" in ancient texts.

Hebrews 13:4 articulates the standard by which Christians were to live in that culture. It tells churches what to teach their members and/or when to intervene to counsel and correct Christians who are compromising the moral standards of the community of faith. In all cases, the issue was not to "clobber" people who were behaving immorally but to protect the sanctity of marriage. The goal was never "heteronormativity" for Christians but moral uprightness. And the desired outcome was not to "overturn public policy" either in Rome or the United States but to foster holiness within the communities of Christ-followers known as churches.

Back to the "Flashing Red Lights"

Do I think the erosion of moral values traced by Gallup in the findings cited above could be stalled and reversed by following this Christian standard? Of course, I do. The more people who are Christians, the fewer incidents of gang violence, riots and looting, drug-related deaths, corporate greed, and homelessness there will be, too. That is why so many of us teach, preach, and write to advance the Christian message. We are attempting to persuade one person here and another there to confess Christ, receive the gift of his saving and transforming grace, and embrace the lifestyle called for in Holy Scripture. We believe lives are richer, families are stronger, and cultures are healthier when Christian truth is more widely believed and followed. But to believe in Christ is to make a personal decision – not something to be imposed against someone's will.

The issue at stake here is not America, capitalism, or social stability. The concern is the Kingdom of God – *Christ's prayer for the will of God to be done on Earth as in Heaven.*

Therefore, this book does not seek to define what courts and legislatures may do to (re)define marriage or permit sexual behaviors the Bible prohibits. Instead, it is a call for Christian leaders to maintain the biblical standards of conduct for ourselves and the souls under our care. It is – even in the face of failed church leadership – a call for all believers to hold ourselves accountable to the authority of Jesus that attaches to Scripture.

What follows in this work, then, is a presentation of what I believe is *orthodox Christian doctrine* about the sanctity of marriage and family and the Christian standard for sexual purity. The specific circumstance that makes this sort of presentation important is that the current social pressures to accept and normalize same-sex unions – giving them equality of status and divine blessing with male-female marriages – seriously misrepresent Scripture and historical data. Those misleading statements and claims have confused many Christians who need better information than they have been given in today's aggressive campaign to lead Christians to "affirm" same-sex marriage. Culture and law may approve, but Scripture does not. Christians should know why we are held to a different standard.

In times past and present, Christians have been disrespectful and harsh toward gay and lesbian persons, family members who "came out," transgender persons, and others from the LGBTQ+ community. I have been guilty, too, and deeply regret it. Homophobia has generated violence against persons made in the image of God. All such behavior is wrong, and Christians must denounce it as against the heart and will of God. The time has come for better communication and more loving behavior. I want this book to contribute to both.

THE LAYOUT OF THIS BOOK

The following material is organized into six studies that address several key issues at stake in the current discussion of same-sex marriage, gender identity, and issues involving the LGBTQ+ community of persons. The chapters are relatively brief and can be explored in much more depth by consulting my larger book titled *Male and Female God Created Them: A Biblical Review of LGBTQ+ Claims*. Anyone planning to teach, lead a discussion group, or who wants details and primary sources around this subject would find the larger volume helpful as a resource and reference work. After each chapter, there are several prompts for reflection and discussion.

Chapter One is my effort to set the thesis and tone for this book. The church's reaction to the larger topic of human sexuality and to the narrower issue of same-sex relationships hasn't always been helpful. It hasn't always been Christlike, in fact. When Jesus faced issues of this sort, he could bring both *grace* and *truth* to the fore. Some contemporary churches have been so "gracious" (in their view) that they turned loose of biblical truth, whereas others have been so determined to uphold "truth" (in their view) that they exhibited very little that could be seen as compassion, kindness, or grace. Churches have gotten so enmeshed in Western civilization's "culture wars" that they have lost sight of their real mission.

Chapter Two insists that the opening pages of the Bible are the correct starting point for understanding human sexuality. Our historic failure to develop a robust theology of human personhood that takes seriously (and positively!) the sexual nature of human beings in God's image has been a serious misfortune to Christian theology and ethics. Our maleness and femaleness are neither evolutionary accidents nor social constructs. We are male and female by divine plan and purpose. Lacking that understanding, human sexuality is easily corrupted. "All You Need Is Love" is more than a song title from the Beatles' music catalog. It has been the romantic sentiment that has driven countless bad decisions across history. God created human beings for relationship, but not every relationship is approved in Scripture and blessed by God.

Chapter Three provides historical and cultural backgrounds that help readers understand how sexuality functioned in the ancient world. That information helps us to read both Old and New Testaments more intelligently. It also puts into perspective the mistaken claim so many people have made to the effect that the biblical writers had no concept of same-sex relationships that were loving, covenantal, and monogamous. Therefore, the argument goes, their moral judgments against same-sex behaviors were meant to address only such perversions as anal rape, master-slave abuse, male prostitution, and – perhaps most specifically – pedophilia and pederasty. To the contrary, historians know that long-term relationships of both male-male and female-female partners are anything but new.

Chapter Four shows from Old Testament literature that same-sex intercourse – regardless of the context of war, idol worship, one-night stand, rape, consent, or covenant – is forbidden in Scripture because it violates both God's creative design for human beings and parodies the one relationship (i.e., male-female marriage) in which genital sex is blessed. It also explores some of the novel twists given to some of the biblical texts in an effort to prove that same-sex unions can be blessed by God. Since every mention of same-sex activity is unequivocally negative in Hebrew Scripture, is it likely that both Jews and Christians have misinterpreted those statements for all these centuries?

Chapter Five moves to the New Testament materials. Is there any sign of an adjustment to or rejection of the consistent Old Testament attitude toward homoerotic behaviors by Jesus, Peter, or Paul? As with recent efforts made by revisionist scholars to amend the reading of Old Testament passages on our subject, there are counter-interpretations of some of these materials as well. How credible are those readings? Should churches move to affirm gay and lesbian relationships? Should churches use their buildings for gay and lesbian commitment ceremonies or permit their ministry staff to officiate them? Are Christians who persist in holding the church's historic position simply "on the wrong side of history"?

Chapter Six attempts to understand why there has been such a rapid change of views on same-sex unions in the past century. Societal-cultural changes tend to take place slowly, but the speed with which Western culture has come to tolerate, legitimate through its courts and legislatures, and normalize gay and lesbian has been nothing short of startling. There are at least five identifiable cultural shifts that have made it possible. In fact, these five movements may have made it inevitable. What they were and how they combined to produce such a rapid 180-degree turn in American culture are traced here.

Because these things are so basic to human relationships, so central to biblical teaching about the moral duties of God's covenant people, and so obviously a part of the standard by which we will be judged on the Last Day, they simply cannot be dismissed as trivial. I sincerely pray that what follows will serve to enlighten, guide, and encourage people who are seeking to know and do the will of God.

How You Might Use This Book

Your primary concern for picking up this book to read may be for personal information. Many Christians are trying to understand the language and practical issues involved in our cultural context. You may be one of those persons. My hope is that you will find clear and helpful information here that assists you in sorting out your own views. What does this or that claim mean? What is the historical or linguistic information needed to evaluate it? How should we treat people with whom we disagree?

Given the likelihood that you know someone who is wrestling with these issues or who has a family member who is gay or lesbian, perhaps you will find this book helpful enough that you will want to share it with that person. Even if it is someone you know holds a different point of view, it can help you focus your conversations. I certainly hope it will help keep the tone of those discussions civil in nature and moderated in tone. From those discussions, it is likely that both of you will come to a clearer understanding of just what is at stake.

There may be a small group in your church or one you participate in already that is raising some of these issues. This book can be a resource to focus a six- or twelve-week study. The questions at the end of each chapter are designed to facilitate discussions in those settings. They will be useful as well in the first two ways suggested for using the book.

Finally, the materials here can be adapted by a youth minister or competent teacher for a series of studies for a church's youth group. Young people in your church are feeling the pressure to adopt the *laissez-faire* attitude of the larger culture toward premarital sex, gender transitioning, same-sex marriage, and the like. We must use both courage and good judgment to give them solid information from Scripture. Don't underestimate what your child or the youth group at your church already knows about sexual matters – and their ability to deal with things discussed here. My fear is that we both undervalue and underestimate the intelligence of young people today. They need reliable information presented by thoughtful teachers on subjects such as this – not juvenile experiences that leave them wondering about things that really matter to them.

If this book whets your appetite to read more deeply and to look more carefully at the data from Bible study, ancient history, linguistic issues, and the like, order a copy of *Male and Female God Created Them: A Biblical Review of LGBTQ+ Claims* from College Press, Amazon, or your local bookstore. It is a far more detailed study than the length of this book permits. By all means, if you plan to be a discussion leader or to teach others from this volume, you need the fuller information contained in *Male and Female God Created Them* to use in your preparation.

May God bless your study of this book and use it to give you helpful insights into Holy Scripture that will be of great value to your spiritual journey.

> *"Now I commit you to God and to the word of his grace, which can build you up and give you an inheritance among all those who are sanctified"* (Acts 20:32).

RUBEL SHELLY

> *To prepare you for what follows in Chapter 1, think about the following excerpt from a respected historian who is an atheist – but who sees the unique contribution of the Christian faith in terms of its teaching about the love of God. While I would quarrel with his comment about "patriarchy," that is for another setting. Here he underscores a central tenet of Christian teaching to be explored in the coming chapter. As an "outsider" to Christianity, his comment is all the more interesting.*

"There is no graded scale of essential worth," [Dr. Martin Luther] King had written a year before his assassination. "Every human being has etched in his personality the indelible stamp of the Creator. Every man must be respected because God loves him." Every woman too, a feminist might have added.

Yet King's words, while certainly bearing witness to an instinctive strain of patriarchy within Christianity, bore witness as well to why, across the Western world, this was coming to seem a problem. That every human being possessed an equal dignity was not remotely self-evident a truth. A Roman would have laughed at it.

To campaign against discrimination on the grounds of gender or sexuality, however, was to depend on large numbers of people sharing in a common assumption: that everyone possessed an inherent worth. The origins of this principle – as Nietzsche had so contemptuously pointed out – lay not in the French Revolution, nor in the Declaration of Independence, nor in the Enlightenment, but in the Bible.

Tom Holland, *Dominion: How the Christian Revolution Remade the World* (New York: Basic Books, 2019), 494.

> *Jesus loves me – this I know,*
> *For the Bible tells me so:*
> *Little ones to him belong,*
> *They are weak, but he is strong.*
>
> – Anna Bartlett Warner

1

Jesus Loves You, This I Know . . .

Three of us were together for lunch and talking about what would become this book. We talked about the need for it, the anticipated readers of it, and its theme. What was likely the most insightful comment in our conversation came in the form of a question.

"What do you think Jesus would do if a person who was lesbian or gay came up and wanted to talk to him?" one of my dining partners asked. Proceeding to answer his own question, he looked at the other two of us and continued. "I think he'd give that person a hug!" he said. "Just a great big hug."

That hasn't been the typical reaction of either parents or preachers who were told by a child or church member, "I'm in love with somebody of my same sex." It hasn't been the standard response to this either: "I'm convinced I am a man who is trapped in a female body." Or to this: "You've always known me as 'Robert,' but I want you to call me 'Rachel' from now on. I am transitioning in my gender identity."

Caught a bit off guard by the question, I looked him in the eyes – with, I'm sure, a bit of surprise showing in mine – and said, "I suppose you could say that is precisely what he did – in a very different cultural setting than ours – when a bunch of guys with rocks at the ready dragged a woman 'caught in the act' before Jesus. They were putting him on the spot about his 'orthodoxy,' but he turned the tables and chose a different starting point. He rescued her from their threats, turned the focus from his orthodoxy to their hypocrisy, and sent the woman home instead of to her grave."

The Bible story in question is the one found in John 8, and we will come back to it in a bit. It's fairly complex at one level. It is marvelously simple at another. *Jesus cared about a woman who was nothing more than a topic for discussion – or, perhaps more correctly, an object of abuse – for some pious religious people in his day.* In the slightly adapted words of the children's song: *Jesus loved her – this I know, for the Bible tells us so.* Those of us who claim to be his followers would do well to learn from his example. And to imitate it.

Culture Wars

You likely know and use the term "culture wars." It is the common way we refer to the ugly divisions and heated language you can witness in a classroom debate over legalizing marijuana, during a political demonstration about gun control, on the editorial page of newspapers about abortion, or when a local church or whole denomination is thinking about expanded roles for women in its leadership structures. At the moment, sexual intercourse between persons of the same sex, gender transitioning, polyamory, gender dysphoria, same-sex marriage, and a host of related topics around what has come to be known as the LGBTQ+ community are front-line engagements in the Western world's culture wars. And they will be for the foreseeable future.

In broadest terms, our culture wars are being fought over everything from music and art to climate change and race relations. The battle lines for these wars are marked variously as liberal vs. conservative, Red State vs. Blue State, "haves" vs. "have-nots," Democrats vs. Republicans, state vs. federal, religious vs. secular, and on and on *ad infinitum*. The ideal in these wars – and "war" is probably the correct term to use of these tensions – is not understanding another's point of view or being respectful toward someone with a different opinion. The goal is *winning*. And, according to an old dictum, "all is fair in love and war." Thus, the language is brutal at city council meetings, in school board discussions, among church leaders, and at family dining tables. There is more shouting than discussion. Acts of physical aggression and harm have come to be commonplace.

Things have gotten so tense on the national political scene that some very serious historians and political scientists are wondering if the American experiment as a democratic republic can survive. A *culture* war typically precedes a *shooting* war. Fortunately, not every culture war ends that way. But it has happened often enough across history that sane and responsible people are begging for people to lower their voices, act with greater civility, and practice the Golden Rule of treating others as you want to be treated.

In the hostile and alienating posture taken by certain right-wing Christian leaders who have aligned themselves with first one and then another political party, no one has been well-served. The Kingdom of God has been reduced to Western nationalism and Christians looked at by the broader public simply as one more voting bloc vying for power. Unbelievers have been handed repeated reasons to be skeptical of – if not adamantly hostile to – the church because of its alignment with corrupt politicians or partisan policies that work against their interests.

Being Christian is not equivalent to being North American or Western. In fact, the most significant spread of the Christian faith as I write this paragraph is in Africa and Asia. The decline in church attendance (i.e., "dechurching" is the term some use to name the phenomenon) and the growth of the "Nones" in America – many of whom have not stopped believing in Jesus but definitely have given up on "institutional church" – should say something to thought leaders in seminaries and pulpits. It doesn't appear that the message is being heard.

The late Tim Keller was bold to warn Christians against identifying the church with either major American political party as having some divine right to lead. Increasingly, however, churches are "red" or "blue" and their pulpits take their cues from political debates and personalities rather than the Gospels and Jesus. To equate loyalty to Jesus with the (fill-in-the-blank) Party is to commit idolatry. Keller was both clear and orthodox when he wrote to this point several years ago in the *New York Times*.

> For example, following both the Bible and the early church, Christians should be committed to racial justice and the poor, but also to the understanding that sex is only for marriage and for nurturing family. One of those views seems liberal and the other looks oppressively conservative. The historical Christian positions on social issues do not fit into contemporary political alignments.[4]

Racism-Poverty and Sex Only in Marriage

Keller's quote names two of the hottest conflicts in our American culture wars.

---

[4] Timothy Keller, "How Do Christians Fit Into the Two-Party System? They Don't," *New York Times*, Sept 29, 2018, https://www.nytimes.com/2018/09/29/opinion/sunday/christians-politics-belief.html.

The church culture in which I grew up was aggressively passive and deafeningly silent about racism and the poverty it perpetuates. Black persons could be denied opportunity, redlined, kept from better-funded White schools, barred from attending White churches, spit on, knocked down by high-pressure water hoses, beaten with nightsticks, attacked by police dogs, and lynched. White pulpits refused to address the issue because it was "social" and "political" rather than spiritual. Neither of the major political parties forced the issue. It was a Baptist preacher writing a letter to silent Christian leaders from a jail cell that pricked many a conscience and helped precipitate change.

Put most simply, the Judeo-Christian faith has political implications but cannot achieve its purposes by posturing itself with a given social structure or political party. Its "political implications" require believers to love our neighbors by caring for the poor, tending to the sick, and being concerned for people in prison (cf. Deut 15:7-11; Matt 25:31-46; Jas 2:14-16). Those obligations were present for Old Testament Israel in the days of its monarchy and when enslaved by Assyrians or Babylonians. They were there for the church under ancient Rome, medieval feudalism, North Korean totalitarianism, British socialism, or American capitalism. In today's United States, people are choosing – or, in many instances, choosing to reject – their church more on the basis of its leanings to a certain political agenda than by its theology.

True to Keller's thesis, Christians from both liberal and conservative denominations who were registered with different political parties began opening their eyes. They realized that racism is a sin because it violates the second commandment of Jesus about loving your neighbor as yourself. It is a distinctive issue of Christian ethics. Believers from liberal churches led their conservative counterparts because of their commitment to improving the human condition – a humanitarian mission with strong biblical support. Conservatives began coming around when some of their respected teachers confessed their prejudice before the biblical text they had silenced – while claiming to defend the faith. It was a sorry season in church history that is still working itself out. Too many vestiges of racism remain yet in too many places where Christians have significant presence and influence.

The second issue Keller named is that "sex is only for marriage" within the context of nurturing children in families. At the time he wrote and even more since then, Western culture has rejected such a view as narrow, old-fashioned, and eccentric. No sense of shame attaches to sex outside marriage or having children without a traditional male-female marital commitment. Even to hint in the direction of calling such behavior morally wrong is deemed "judgmental" and "hateful." Sexual intercourse is no longer considered a privilege of marriage but simply a form of recreation. What was once regarded as the most intimate of human interactions is now called "casual sex" or "just sex." So long as there is consent, according to the majority Western view, there is nothing wrong with hooking up or simply living together. For some, sex is admittedly more a sport than a bonding experience within marriage, more a personal right than an element of sacred covenantal commitment.

Most recently, what began as the gay liberation movement of the late 1960s has been validated by courts and legislatures with the legal redefinition of marriage itself. The claim has been made successfully that – since Western cultural practice had come to accept sex as a personal right to pleasure – there is no consistent basis for rejecting same-sex coupling. A well-orchestrated strategy for normalizing same-sex partnerships was outlined in a 1989 book[5] that many have dubbed the "public relations manual for the gay agenda." The strategy outlined there has worked to characterize

---

[5] Marshall Kirk and Hunter Madsen, *After the Ball: How America Will Conquer Its Fear and Hatred of Gays in the '90s* (New York: Plume Books, 1989).

orthodox Christian faith as bigotry and the church as out of step with today's world. The American Psychiatric Association removed homosexuality from its list of mental disorders in 1973. Television sitcoms and celebrity lifestyles have removed it from public disfavor. The issue is no longer *toleration* of alternative lifestyles but their *affirmation* as altogether acceptable and morally respectable – perhaps, as one website puts it, "the ultimate expression of your true self." And the church has often reacted poorly.

Liberal churches have continued their established policy of affirming human experience as having greater authority than an ancient document such as the Bible. And conservative churches met the 1960s and its sexual revolution with outrage and fiery bombast – rather than compassion and loving discourse. And that brings me back to my account of the table discussion at the top of this chapter.

Jesus Brings BOTH Grace AND Truth

Is it unthinkable to you that Jesus would give a great big hug to someone who wanted to talk with him about same-sex issues – perhaps simply to put that person's fears to rest? Just recall how John opens his Gospel. In the prologue, he affirms that the Eternal Logos has become flesh. God had been revealing his life-giving oral word across the centuries through various prophets such as Moses, Israel's great lawgiver. In Jesus, however, that word became flesh. If we use English linguistic protocols to summarize it, the word became The Word. The truth became The Truth. Lower-case *concepts* became upper-case *Divine Presence*. "The Law was given through Moses," John reminds us, "grace and truth came through Jesus Christ" (John 1:17).

John's statement should never be read as a statement meant to diminish the Law of Moses. All that came through Moses was from the God who has made himself known as both the source of truth and also a never-ending fountain of grace. Thus, we read both "I, the LORD, speak the truth" (Isa 45:19) and "You, Lord, are a compassionate and gracious God, slow to anger, abounding in love and faithfulness" (Psa 86:15). What had been communicated and mediated through Moses was brought to its ideal fulfillment in the Logos who took on flesh. What humans had heard about and glimpsed in various settings was now both complete and permanently present in Israel's Messiah – here not only for Israel but also for all who believe in him. Grace and truth now have a name and address in space-time history – *Jesus of Nazareth*.

What we see in John 8, then, is a case study of how grace and truth function. First, there was grace to spare a woman whom some were wanting to put to death. Jesus showed compassion and love to her by forcing the hand of her accusers – who obviously had conspired to trap her in order to ambush Jesus. If she was a mere pawn in a power game for them, she was a person in Jesus' eyes. Jesus knew there was more to the Torah than occasional death sentences for the most severe of ethical-spiritual offenses.

Under the Law his enemies claimed to be upholding, the Torah imposed strict accountability on would-be witnesses. It is especially harsh with anyone who is a "malicious witness" – someone who knowingly gives false testimony or who has been party to the offense in question. (There was no such thing as "turning state's evidence" under the Law of Moses.) He would bring on himself the penalty his false declaration would have imposed on the person about whom he had given contrived and false testimony (Deut 19:15-19). When the men who were trying to ambush Jesus and the woman realized *they* were the ones who had been caught in a snare, they dropped their stones and decided it was time to go home.

Alone now with a woman who had committed a serious sexual sin that could have brought the death penalty to her, Jesus didn't give her a physical hug – as that would have been improper for a rabbi of that time and place. He did, however, give her what amounted to one with these words: "Then neither do I condemn you" – for he had not witnessed the woman's sin and could not give evidence against her. Then he followed his verbal hug with this challenge: "Go now and leave your life of sin" (John 8:11).

Grace and *truth!* And, please, notice the order in which John named the two in John 1 and how Jesus exhibits them in John 8. In most settings of my life experience, wounded, misbehaving, and sinful people need grace before they can receive truth. *Truth is fundamental, but without grace it is too demanding to be heard – much less embraced and lived.*

If Jesus could show grace without compromising truth and uphold truth without distorting grace, surely that is what those of us who wear his name should attempt to do. Indeed, that is the goal of this book. I want to make a clear and positive case for the historic and universal view of the Christian church that sexual intercourse is reserved for monogamous male-with-female marriage. That responsibility will require me to show why adultery, premarital sex, and same-sex intercourse are outside God's will and sinful. But I want to make that case in a spirit of love and grace. I will show respect for the personhood, dignity, and intelligence of anyone willing to read this book in the process.

Every human being has been created in God's own image. As her Creator's image-bearer, she should not be subjected to dehumanizing catcalls, sexual harassment, or violence. As someone loved by God, he should not be insulted, mocked, or denigrated. As strongly as the advocates of same-sex union with whom I disagree, I join them in denouncing the verbal or physical attacks against gay, lesbian, transgender, or other persons in the LGBTQ+ community – or their straight sympathizers. If the people filled with anger and threats against gay or transgender persons are "dead right" in their reading of the Bible, they are "dead wrong" to dehumanize and abuse other human beings.

What This Book Does Not Argue

This book isn't about politics, economics, or even the broader issue of religious vs. secular value systems. I don't have any meaningful voice in those arenas. I am a Christian theologian and have no right to force (as if that were remotely possible!) my distinctly Christian views on people who are not Christians. Yes, Christians should be good citizens, participate in public life, and use our influence for the common good. But the recent wave of "Christian Nationalism" that has tried to write biblical distinctives into civil statutes is *un*biblical on its surface.

When Joseph was sold into slavery in Egypt only to wind up 13 years later as the sole person Pharaoh had put "in charge of the whole land of Egypt" (Gen 41:41), he did not use his position to set up alternate sites of worship to Yahweh. When Daniel was carried off to Babylon in 606 B.C. and made a civil servant in its government (Dan 1:3-5, 18-21), he served well for decades without exploiting the political system to enact the Torah's ethical demands – which were very different from the traditions of the Babylonians. The social-political strategy of God's people in the larger Babylonian context was that they should settle, establish families, and "seek the peace and prosperity" of their new environment. Above all, they were to "pray to the Lord for it" as resident aliens in a foreign culture (Jer 29:5-7). As they did so, they were bearing witness to the True God by living as a righteous people in an unrighteous environment. In the words of another prophet, they were to live there as "a light for the Gentiles" (Isa 49:6b).

Christians have the right to voice our convictions on issues of concern for the common good. But our arguments in the public square must be based on shared values and rational argument. Why should we expect the secular, non-Christian people around us to be bound by the distinctive elements of our faith? Isn't that as unfair as the dictates we decry in Saudi Arabia, Afghanistan, or various Gulf States where Islamic Sharia law is imposed on Christians and other non-Muslims?

There will be no ranting here against the courts and legislatures for the actions they have taken over the past few decades to disallow blue laws, protect the privacy of gay and lesbian partners, or even the hard-to-fathom redefinition of "marriage" to include same-sex unions – however much I may disagree with one or more of those moves. There is no strategy here for striking down one or more of the revised laws that have created expanded rights. It is not the business of churches to write a nation's civil laws, punish those who offend, or otherwise regulate the lives of our neighbors who do not believe the Bible.

Both Christians and non-Christians may link arms in certain situations, for example, to argue against transgender participation in athletic competition. Few are the mothers or fathers of a female athlete who want their daughter who has two X chromosomes to compete with a larger, more muscular high school or college athlete with one X and one Y chromosome. Multiple scientific studies have shown that trans-female athletes have significant physical advantages (e.g., greater muscle mass, strength, running speed) over their peers who were born female.[6] For that matter,

---

[6] Alison K. Heather, "Transwoman Elite Athletes: Their Extra Percentage Relative to Female Physiology," *International Journal of Environmental Research and Public Health*, vol. 19,15 (July 26, 2022): 9103, accessed May 26, 2023, at https://www.ncbi.nlm.nih.gov/pmc/articles/PMC9331831/pdf/ijerph-19-09103.pdf; cf. Ari Blaff, "NPR *Issues Correction, Admits There Is Evidence Proving Male Athletes Have Advantage over Females*," Mar 27, 2023, accessed May 26, 2023, at https://www.nationalreview.com/news/npr-claims-limited-scientific-evidence-men-have-physical-advantage-over-women-in-sports.

what of that same daughter in high school having to use restrooms with trans persons or graduating and entering a workplace where laws have had to be passed to protect females – laws that no longer can be enforced?[7] Athletics and workplace laws are not biblical mandates unique to believers.

Similarly, Christians – along with Muslims, atheists, and other citizens – may have good medical and psychological reasons for opposing what some term "gender-affirming care." This approach to treating children with gender dysphoria with puberty-blocking drugs and/or genital surgeries at 16 or 13 or even younger ages is being questioned seriously on clinical grounds. England's National Health Service recently has restricted the use of puberty blockers to clinical trials because "there is not enough evidence to support their safety or clinical effectiveness as a routinely available treatment." Sweden – long a precedent-setting leader in gender-affirming care – took a significant step in 2022. Its national health care oversight body, after a systematic review, declared "the risks of puberty-inhibiting and gender-affirming hormone treatment for those under 18 currently outweigh the possible benefits." Some American clinicians are calling now for such a systematic review of policies and practices in this country.

In a period of Christendom when churches had wide-ranging power to influence public policy, things such as daily Bible reading or (Christian) prayers in public schools were put in place. Our non-Christian neighbors resented those intrusions into their lives. How did we ever misunderstand the teaching from Paul in 1 Corinthians 5:9-13? He instructed Christians living in a Greco-Roman city whose culture was self-indulgent and depraved that they should be a community of alternate values in its midst – as the captives in Babylon were called

---

[7] Colin M. Wright and Emma N. Hilton, "The Dangerous Denial of Sex," *Wall Street Journal*, Feb 13, 2020, accessed at https://www.wsj.com/articles/the-dangerous-denial-of-sex-11581638089.

to be in Jeremiah's appeal. He specifically said, however, that they were not to judge sexually immoral, greedy, or false religious beliefs *outside* their fellowship. *The Message* translates his counsel this way: "I'm not responsible for what the *outsiders* do, but don't we have some responsibility within our community of believers?" (1 Cor 5:12).

The United States of America is not the Kingdom of God. Neither is Canada, Sweden, nor Italy. There are no geographical boundaries that contain or describe it. For our country, neither Democrats nor Republicans nor Independents can be looked to for our salvation. The church can confess only one Lord Jesus Christ, worship only one God the Father, and find empowerment to live holy lives from the one Holy Spirit. Looking elsewhere is nothing less than *idolatry* – a subject we will return to later in this book.

This book is written to teach, counsel, and appeal to Christians. It lays out a case for sexual purity in this chaotic culture that non-Christians can neither appreciate nor embrace. Its foundation is the confession "Jesus is Lord!" and it accepts the biblical teaching that our bodies belong to God and are temples of the Holy Spirit. This confession and belief combine to bring one to embrace certain positive (e.g., kindness, patience, self-giving love) and negative (e.g., rejecting greed, lust, sexual immorality) moral virtues as behaviors we seek to embody on a daily basis.

Can one be orthodox in faith and moral in behavior who believes, practices, defends, and/or teaches same-sex intimacy is a way of life approved by God? Authorized by Scripture? Acceptable within a community of faithful Christians?

As You Read . . .

As you read this book, please keep a couple of things in mind.

First, terminology is always a problem in discussing LGBTQ+ topics. For example, the *nouns* "homosexual" and "homosexuality" are tricky. On the one hand, they may refer to a state of mind (i.e., inclination, disposition) or a lived experience (i.e., sexual intercourse, same-sex marriage). In this book, I will avoid using either term as a noun to avoid this confusion.

One's feelings for or romantic inclinations in relation to persons of the same sex is not sinful in itself. Nurtured as lust or acted out as same-sex behavior is what the Bible forbids. As I will argue later, the issue is the act itself and not some predisposition or genetic orientation to the act. Therefore, I will use the word "homosexual" as an *adjective* at various points to speak of homosexual behavior or homosexual relationships. This distinction is my attempt to follow the biblical usage, where its negative judgment is against same-sex actions rather than same-sex orientation. *It is conduct rather than sentiment or inclination that is at stake in the biblical text.* This points to a critical distinction for us to make between *orientation* and *activity*.

So, yes, this will sometimes generate cumbersome phrasing such as "same-sex intercourse" or "same-sex behavior" where someone else might use the word "homosexuality" or describe a person as "homosexual." But I respect Christian men and women of my acquaintance who describe themselves as "chaste persons who are same-sex attracted" as opposed to their "sexually active gay friends"– just as there are "chaste straight people" and "sexually active heterosexual persons" in my circle of acquaintance. This evolved and more nuanced distinction between attitudes and actions has created the recent muddled claims about the 1946 edition of the Revised Standard Version.

Second, this book is written with a minimum of technical terms and footnote references. When some technical term is introduced, I will try always to give the working definition being used for it here. But, as you would expect, there will be some foreign words (usually Hebrew or Greek) and even English terms (such as the distinction between sex and gender) that will appear in the text. As to footnotes, they will be rather meager for the simple reason that most people don't care for them and are distracted by them. There is a much larger book I have written on this subject titled *Male and Female God Created Them*[8] that has detailed footnotes and scholarly references into both original and secondary sources for those who really want to dig deeply into this material on their own.

THE PLATFORM FOR THIS BOOK

Returning once more to the big-hug conversation related in the introduction to this chapter, let me remind you of the words of the children's song most of us know by heart. That "Jesus Loves Me" is the beginning point for this study.

Regardless of your opinions or life situation relative to same-sex practices, I am writing in the absolute confidence that "Jesus Loves YOU – this I know, / For the Bible tells us so." In the love of Jesus, there is the constant desire for those who profess faith in him to follow his steps of obedience to his Father's will. His call to me as a sinner has required repentance in multiple settings.

His "Follow me!" call to anyone involved in either heterosexual or homosexual behaviors that are outside the Father's will as made known in the Bible will involve repentance. That means that anyone who is sexually active with another person outside the covenant commitment of one man and one woman in marriage is challenged to put Jesus above all others by repenting, accepting God's gracious pardon, and receiving the daily strength of the Holy Spirit to live a chaste life.

Sexual morality is not the heart of the gospel message. Sexual purity is not a means to earning one's salvation. Sexual sin should not be classed as somehow patently worse than all other sins. The

---

[8] Rubel Shelly, *Male and Female God Created Them: A Biblical Review of LGBTQ+ Claims* (Joplin, MO: College Press, 2023).

gospel is the good news that Jesus has opened the way to redemption and life through his death, burial, and resurrection. Salvation is by God's abundant grace through our often-anemic faith. That faith is dead, however, unless it shows itself in a living faith that exhibits an authentic transformation of a person's life.

When Paul wrote an epistle to the Christ-followers in Colossae, he replied to a "hollow and deceptive philosophy" (Col 2:8) that was leading some away from the faith. We don't know the name or specifics of that philosophy, but it clearly offered some sort of inside track to spiritual life through legalistic rules and rituals "based on merely human commands and teachings" (cf. 2:20-23). How common this has been in church history! The people pushing this self-help program of rigid tenets had "lost connection with the head" (Christ as the source of identity and life) and offered a system of "harsh" self-restraint that "lack[ed] any value in restraining sensual indulgence" – the sort of sexual permissiveness that was an accepted fact of life in the Greco-Roman world of Paul's time.

Paul's response to the Colossian problem was not to cancel the Judeo-Christian call to sexual purity. It was to insist they were trying to do a right and proper thing (i.e., restrain sensual indulgence) by a wrong and improper method (i.e., submitting to rigid rule-keeping under some form of strict supervision). This sounds a lot like the cultic Christian groups that have formed on university campuses to keep students out of "the party life" that tends to dominate. Rigid rules enforced by human monitors of behavior may seem to work for a while but generally wind up in spiritual burnout – a burnout so severe that it often destroys faith.

Paul's alternate solution is the one to be offered in this book. One writer sums up Paul's approach this way: "Rules must never take the place of Christ as the source of spiritual nourishing and growth; and any rules that we propose to follow must be clearly rooted in and lead back to Christ."⁹ If someone's intrusive "System of Dos and Don'ts" – like the best-selling *I Kissed Dating Goodbye* book, DVD series, and church-conferences of the early 2000s that hurt so many people and led to spiritual disaster for its author – isn't the solution, then what is?

Paul offers a compelling and positive vision of a new type of life "in Christ" that rigid religion and its oppressive piling up of *rules* on top of *more rules* on top of *still more rules* simply cannot fathom. It is light years distant from the legalistic forms of Christian faith that give people they may designate as "mentors" or "spiritual guides" the right to monitor, pry, and regulate your behaviors. It sounds astonishingly simple.

> Since, then, you have been raised with Christ, set your hearts on things above, where Christ is, seated at the right hand of God. Set your minds on things above, not on earthly things. For you died, and your life is now hidden with Christ in God. When Christ, who is your life, appears, then you also will appear with him in glory (Col 3:1-4).

The Christian faith is not a system. It is not a dos-and-don'ts program for escaping Hell. It is a relationship with Jesus Christ that changes your focus for living. It redirects your life goal from earthly to heavenly concerns. *It is a mental, emotional, physical, total-person reorientation of your life that changes everything.*

Jesus compared the experience to a pearl merchant finding a single pearl of such quality and value that he sold everything else he had to purchase it (Matt 13:45-46). For himself, Paul described it this way: "I have been crucified with Christ and I no longer live, but Christ lives in me" (Gal 2:20). Or, in another place, using language that sounds a bit similar to Jesus' parable about someone cashing in everything he owns for a single priceless pearl: "Whatever were

---

⁹ Douglas J. Moo, *The Letters to the Colossians and to Philemon* (Grand Rapids: Eerdmans, 2008), 70.

gains to me I now consider loss for the sake of Christ. What is more, I consider everything a loss because of the surpassing worth of knowing Christ Jesus my Lord, for whose sake I have lost all things" (Phil 3:7-8a).

For people who have not yet experienced it, this sort of language has to sound strange. It must sound mystical and beyond reach to some. Why, it may just sound so far-fetched as to be crazy to their ears. I get it. But, referring back to the report of Tim Keller's death in a secular newspaper, it is interesting that he is quoted on the point of his understanding that sex is only for marriage in a previous *New York Times* interview. I tracked down that article – only to find Keller making the point I want you to hear now. It was in a news story covering the unlikely connection a conservative Christian could make with New Yorkers.

> Mr. Keller has managed to make a pull-no-punches Christianity credible to his congregation by packaging conservative theology in a nonjudgmental style. He does not dictate personal behavior or politics in his sermons. Instead, he talks about people choosing the right path because of their spiritual connection to God. "I am not going to pressure you to stop having sex out of marriage," he says, for example. "The logic of your relationship with Christ should move you to do it."[10]

Did you catch the critical line of that quote? It is "the logic of your relationship with Christ" that makes it unnecessary for some human to dictate your life choices. While there is a "nonjudgmental style" in Colossae or Rome, New York or Los Angeles that prohibits some onstage church personality from piling up man-made rules to crush you, following Jesus creates the desire to hear God's voice as it marks the boundaries within which his children live. Following Jesus means – among other things – rejecting what he called "merely

---

[10] Edward Lewine, "Making New Christians," *New York Times*, Jan 25, 1998, https://www.nytimes.com/1998/01/25/nyregion/making-new-christians.html.

human rules" to follow the Scriptures (Matt 15:9; cf. 5:19). *Human systems enslave; God's reign liberates.*

But I'm getting ahead of myself. This book will explore the logic of a relationship with Christ that not only acknowledges but also finds the deep motivation and strength to live by the teaching of Scripture. At various points in this study, the work of the Holy Spirit will be part of the discussion. It is only the Spirit's power that enables you or me to live the life Paul was celebrating in the opening verses of Colossians 3. That chapter proceeds, by the way, to talk about biblical commands – both negative and positive ones – in terms of taking off an old wardrobe and replacing it with a brand new one that is far more attractive (Col 3:5-14).

Without being judgmental, Paul is quite specific in naming the evil things that must go and the holy behaviors that will emerge in the lives of people living out the logic of their relationship with Christ. It is done best, he says, in a supportive community (i.e., the church) of others who are thinking, talking, and praying for the same outcomes (Col 3:15-17). He even explains some of the short-term demands that will be made on believers in the interim between our spiritual conversion to Christ and his personal return to set all things right – whether within skewed family dynamics or in relation to such evils as human slavery (Col 3:18-4:6)

Conclusion

For those of us who have committed ourselves to Jesus as Lord, knowing and doing the will of God is fundamental. But that doesn't sanction some sort of mean-spirited legalism that has you being judged harshly by others so you can turn around and judge someone else with an equal or greater severity. It is about understanding the meaning of being in Christ and having Christ in us. It is learning to live by the logic of Jesus – that actually turns the dictates of Heaven into the desires of our hearts. By the power of the Spirit of God, all things become new.

So we begin our study – knowing *for sure* that Jesus loves us. He loves *all* of us. We begin, too, with a commitment to love him back by following Jesus within the revealed will of his Heavenly Father – and ours.

Finally, there will be occasional hints and sometimes specific challenges for churches to provide more for our single members than most do. Single people – whether never married, divorced, or widowed – are complete and whole persons before God. They should not be treated as outliers in family-oriented (i.e., mom, dad, and the kids) churches. And we certainly need to demonstrate more love and support for those with same-sex orientation. They are not lepers among us who need to be quarantined but persons in need of practical help – along with their brothers and sisters of heterosexual orientation – to walk uprightly before God.

With an initial literary hug exchanged between us now, we begin our study. Let's begin – as we always should in studying Holy Scripture – with a prayer for God's blessing and help.

> *Holy Triune God, as we begin this study, we plead for your guidance. Let us hear your Holy Word – even when it challenges us, makes us uncomfortable, or calls for a change in the way we have been thinking and living. By the presence and power of the Holy Spirit, mold us into the likeness of our Lord Jesus Christ. Renew our minds to think with the logic of Jesus that will move us to seek and do what honors you. For yours is the kingdom, power, and glory forever. Amen.*

1

Questions for Reflection

THINK ABOUT . . .
THE PLIGHT OF THE JEWS IN BABYLON

This chapter refers to the 70 years of Babylonian Exile (606-536 BC) for the Jewish people. God's people lived as sojourners in exile from their home. They were challenged to be a blessing to their captors – while modeling the distinctive faith to which Abraham and his offspring had been called. How does this serve as a precedent for Christians today in Cuba, North Korea, China, or the United States?

EXPLORE . . .
1 PETER 2:11-17

Do you hear an echo of the *exile* theme in these verses? 1 Peter is an extended call for early Christians to live as Christ-followers in the unfriendly spiritual-moral climate of the Roman Empire. What is Peter's negative appeal? His positive challenge? Why do you think he did not call for Christians to withdraw into monastic communities? Simply cut themselves off from the social pressures of the empire?

PRACTICE . . .
LIVING AS RESIDENT ALIENS

In Babylonian Exile, under Roman rule in the first century, or in your life situation today, anyone who is faithful to God will wind up living as a *resident alien* in his or her culture. This means that Christians must be careful not to get too comfortable with our culture's values. Our mission is to be agents of redemption in the world.

1. In your own words, define the status of "resident alien" in today's culture.
2. What resources do you draw from to remind you of your relationship to the world's values?
3. How do you avoid letting the world's negative stereotype of the Christian faith make you into a reactionary person – a negative, cranky, judgmental soul? Have you ever lapsed into that sort of behavior out of frustration?
4. How does this chapter's focus on *grace and truth* shed light on your life as a resident alien?
5. Summarize Tim Keller's comments on "the logic of a relationship with Christ." Do you agree?
6. What is your most important takeaway from Chapter One?

Chapter 2 points to the critical importance of placing everything the Bible says about sexuality in the context of a theology of God's good creation. The following snippet highlights the importance of the Bible's creation story to sexual experience.

The place to start [thinking about sex] is with the telos for which God created us, and why God made the other creatures and us sexual beings: "Be fruitful and multiply" (Genesis 1:22, 28). This tells us that sex, sexual desire, and orgasms are good. Chastity wants us to think about what good it is that they were created for. How do they fit within God's plan for us to love one another and honor God?

The virtue of chastity calls us, as sexual beings, to revere ourselves as creatures made in the image of God and made to honor God through our actions – through how we do have sex and do not have sex.

Matt Fradd, "Chastity as a Virtue," from The Institute of Faith and Learning at Baylor University, 36-37. Accessed at https://ifl.web.baylor.edu/sites/g/files/ecbvkj771/files/2022-11/ChastityArticleFradd.pdf.

> *The creation story underscores the conviction that the drama is not just about human beings; rather, it is a "cosmic journey" that has its beginning and end in the purpose of God.*
> – Bernhard W. Anderson

2

This Goes Back to Eden

Despite the impression some appear to have that sex is an exciting new discovery, it has been around for a long, long time now. Otherwise, you and I wouldn't be trying to figure out what is happening in the values and behavior shift of the last 50 years or so.

Sex in the broader animal creation is for reproduction. It makes babies and keeps species from dying out. Humans are no different from other living creatures in that regard. Without the ability to produce offspring, species *homo sapiens* would simply disappear. We would join dinosaurs, passenger pigeons, and countless other extinct species.

However, while procreation is fundamental to species survival, sexual expression among human beings is significantly more multi-faceted than with the animal population in general. Because we have not only an instinct for survival but also higher intelligence, complex social skills, and ever-changing cultural norms, sexual acts are central to loving nuclear families, romance novels, human trafficking, violence, religion, pornography, law, art, child abuse, exploitation, and . . . Okay. I'm sure you get the point.

Human beings link practically *everything* to sex. Some of the contexts for human sexual bonding are tender, loving, and healthy. Others are sadistic, dehumanizing, and immoral. Between those extremes, we raise questions and have doubts about certain behaviors. Should parents choose and arrange one's marital-sexual partner? Should there be age, class, or religious restrictions? Does covenantal marriage make it wrong to have additional sex partners – if one's mate consents and/or the couple's culture allows it?

To deny that humans are sexual beings is to deny the obvious; to make sexuality the focus of a one's identity and experience begs the question of biblical personhood. The species cannot survive without sex. One can be fully human, however, without the experience of sexual intercourse. As this chapter will argue, the critical issue to a theology of human identity is not sex but *personhood* within the purpose and revealed will of God.

People in the twenty-first century have different vocabularies than ancient civilizations for all aspects of human sexual experience. But there is little – if anything – we can call "new" about it. As far back as we have any ancient drawings or literary fragments, humans have displayed our fascination with sex. Some of those ancient sources describe not only passion but also commitment and constancy most of us would admire. Others are risqué, coarse, and exploitative – one modern term could be pornographic – in nature; they reduce persons into toys for amusement or objects for abuse. So, I repeat: *There is very little about human sexual experience that can be called "new."*

In the recent public discussion of same-sex[11] relationships and the radical change in both their public acceptance and legal status, some irresponsibly mistaken statements have been made that are then cited as facts. Specifically, it is not unusual to hear the claim that committed, long-term relationships between loving partners of the same sex were simply unknown in antiquity – that they are the "new" thing about sex. Thus, the argument goes, when the Bible speaks so emphatically against same-sex partnerships, it must be passing a moral judgment on rape, pederasty,[12] pedophilia,[13] master-slave sexual abuse, prostitution, or perhaps some type of offensive pagan fertility rite.

As a result of these revisionist claims, you read such unequivocal statements as this one: "There are no ancient examples of lifelong, monogamous same-sex relationships between social equals, and certainly none that have societal support."[14] The inaccuracy of that statement will be demonstrated in Chapter Three. Such relationships are *not* "new" at all and were, to the contrary, quite clearly known in antiquity and consistently condemned in the Bible.

---

[11] This book avoids using the word "homosexual" as a noun. The word may mean either (a) someone whose orientation or primary desire is for persons of the same sex or (b) a person who is sexually active with someone of the same sex. Since same-sex *desire* is not the same as same-sex *activity*, I will use the more unwieldy term "same-sex activity." As an adjective, "homosexual *behavior*" or "homosexual *activity*" may be used on occasion. *Note: Some quotations cited may not make the same distinction.*

[12] In Ancient Greece, pederasty (Gk, *paiderastia*) was an approved "social institution" among wealthy families that – while involving sexual activity between older (Gk, *erastēs*) and younger (Gk, *erōmenos*) males – was accepted without shame as a means of education for young men between the approximate ages of 12 and 20 and introduced them to their mentors' professions and circles of political influence. In English, the word means sexual activity between an adult male and a boy.

[13] Pedophilia is typically defined either as a psychological disorder or perversion in which an adult directs his or her sexual fantasies, attentions, and/or actions toward a prepubescent child. It would have been considered inappropriate in ancient as well as modern cultures.

[14] "The Christian tradition doesn't address sexual orientation," *The Reformation Project*, https://reformationproject.org/case/tradition. The Reformation Project defines its mission this way: "As a Bible-based, Christian organization, The Reformation Project's mission is to advance LGBTQ inclusion in the church." TRP was founded by Matthew Vines, whose affirmative case for same-sex marriage was made originally in the book *God and the Gay Christian: The Biblical Case in Support of Same-Sex Relationships* (New York: Convergent Books, 2014). Because my larger book, *Male and Female God Created Them: A Biblical Review of LGBTQ+ Claims*, deals with these issues in relation to three primary writers – David Gushee, Adam Hamilton, and Mark Achtemeier – this shorter treatment will more often use Vine's case from the TRP website and his original book for reference to affirming arguments.

For now, though, it is important that we begin by setting the issue of human sexuality in its biblical context.

The Biblical Setting: Male/Female/One Flesh

From the opening lines of the Bible, who you and I were created to be as humans and how we are to understand our sexual natures as men and women in God's own image is narrated in very clear language. It has been only in the past half century or so that serious challenges have been made to the traditional interpretation of the Bible's case for marriage as the covenantal union within which one male and one female come together with God's blessing to create new life (i.e., produce and rear children) and bear the image of God into his good creation. This recent take on the biblical account is clearly – as its own advocates style it – a "revisionist" point of view.

It is important for us to "begin at the beginning" for at least two reasons.

First, the Bible displays a *positive view of human sexuality*. To focus on a limited number of texts that prohibit prostitution, adultery, or same-sex acts misses the point of why they are found in your Bible. The Bible is neither uneasy about nor negative toward sex. That we are male and female in our human personhood is not an evolutionary accident but a divine plan. The Creator allows his image-bearers to be procreators as part of their likeness to him. Prohibitions related to sexual expression are not for the purpose of denying minorities their rights. To the contrary, they are boundary-markers to protect the divine ideal of male-with-female partnership in nurturing family relationships where sex serves both its fundamental (reproductive) purpose and further bonds and deepens the covenant fidelity the original pair pledges to one another.

Second, the Genesis account of human *commonality* ("bone of my bones and flesh of my flesh") and *difference* ("she shall be called 'woman' because she was taken out of man") is repeatedly looked upon in all the Bible as the norm for marriage. In the Old Testament, Yahweh is the bridegroom to his bride Israel (Isa 54:5; Jer 31:31-32). In the New Testament, the church is the bride of Christ (Eph 5:22-23) – and is moving toward the great marriage feast yet to come at his return (Rev 19:1-14). When asked a question about divorce, Jesus took his questioners back to Genesis by asking, "Haven't you read that at the beginning the Creator 'made them male and female,' and said, 'For this reason a man will leave his father and mother and be united to his wife, and the two will become one flesh'?" (Matt 19:4).

Vines offers a take on the term "one flesh" to make it mean "kinship" and "basic commonality as two people forming a new kinship bond."[15] He is confident "the meaning of the phrase doesn't require gender difference."[16] "What seems to me to be most important in marriage is not whether the partners are anatomically different from one another," he writes. "It's whether the inherently different people involved are willing to keep covenant with each other in a relationship of mutual self-giving."[17] If he is correct that the essence of marriage is (a) commonality without regard to difference and (b) mutual self-giving, the door has not only been opened to same-sex marriage but also to incest, bisexual marriage, and polygamy. There is, in fact, on Vines' view of what constitutes one-flesh union more biblical warrant for polygamy than for same-sex marriage.

Vines cannot appeal to Genesis, for "one flesh" there unquestionably involves sexual differentiation. When the man awakes in the creation account, he said, "This is now bone of my bones and flesh of my flesh [commonality, kinship]; she shall

---
[15] Vines, *God and the Gay Christian*, 144.
[16] Ibid., 146.
[17] Ibid., 147.

be called 'woman,' for she was taken out of man [difference, distinction]" (Gen 2:23). Maleness/masculinity and femaleness/femininity are integral to personhood. They are equally enriching to the other, and each gives to the other a fuller understanding of himself/herself. Neither can Vines appeal to Leviticus, for he argues elsewhere that Israel's Holiness Code is not binding on Christians. As we will see later, this would come as a shocking revelation to New Testament writers who are steeped in the Torah and quote it as having moral authority over Christ's followers.

In this chapter, then, we shall revisit the biblical creation story and then proceed to show how ancient people attempted to manipulate the divine norm into a number of variations – including what we now call "same-sex marriage."

> Creation is *not* just the disposable backdrop to the lives of human creatures who were really intended to live somewhere else, and some day will do so. We are not redeemed *out of* creation, but as *part of* the redeemed creation itself – a creation that will again be fully and eternally for God's glory, for our joy and benefit, and forever.[18]

THE CREATION NARRATIVE

As the biblical story begins, the first five days of creation make Planet Earth habitable for the human beings who are going to be created to bear the divine image into it. So, on the sixth day, "God created mankind [humans, NRSVue] in his own image, in the image of God he created them; male and female he created them" (Gen 1:27). After that wide-angle portrait of creation, the zoomed-in shot adds: "The Lord God formed a man from the dust of the ground and breathed into his nostrils the breath of life, and the man became a living being" (Gen 2:7).

---

[18] Christopher J.H. Wright, *The Mission of God's People: A Biblical Theology of the Church's Mission* (Grand Rapids: Zondervan, 2010), 56.

Two important facts come to light here. First, humans are created in the act of being *embodied*. Unlike non-biblical creation accounts such as that of the Greeks, we are not already existing spirit-beings who have been deposited temporarily into physical bodies. Remember Plato's famous Allegory of the Cave? In his view, humans are "trapped" or "imprisoned" in physical bodies and yearn to be free in order to ascend to divine heights of enlightenment. Or is the Cartesian dualism of mind-body interaction more familiar than Plato? (Too much of both of these theories infect the thinking of contemporary Christians!)

In the biblical account, we are either inspirited bodies or embodied spirits – whichever term you prefer – and are fully human *persons* only in that fused and bonded form. We do not *have* bodies; we *are* bodies quickened to life by our conjoined spirits. Death occurs when the body (i.e., physical, visible part) and spirit (i.e., nonphysical, invisible part) are separated – only to await their reintegration in a bodily resurrection when Christ returns (cf. Jas 2:26a; 1 Cor 15:35ff). *Bodies matter. Bodies are essential to human identity. The human forms we have now will be raised as renewed and imperishable bodily forms that will be suited for life in what the Bible calls the New Heaven and New Earth.*

Second, since the body is irreducibly critical to human form, identity, and activity, the conscious and mindful actions of every human body are at the heart of our moral agency. In other words, what we do in our mortal bodies is always a matter of moral accountability to the God who created it. It actually matters. Decisions about our choices and actions in particular situations are questions about who we are. Right and wrong, good and evil – these are real categories of human behavior.

Over against the modern notion of radical autonomy ("It's *my* body and nobody can tell me what to do with it!") stands the biblical view that a Christian is one whose very *body belongs to God and is a temple of the Holy Spirit*. The biblical calling is thus quite clear and absolute: "Therefore honor God with your bodies" (1 Cor 6:19-20). Our bodies are not our means to erotic pleasure or the psychic comfort of kinship bonding in love. They serve God's kingdom and his righteousness above sentiment, orientation, or culture.

We will come back to this opening biblical theme of the *importance of the human body* when we get to the matter of sex and gender. For now, this much seems to be a reasonable thesis: *bodies are not pliable and fluid to one's mind, spirit, or personality. To the contrary, bodies are of primary importance, and the bodily sex of male or female is a "given" – not an arbitrary "assignment" at birth or a "choice" one can make later along an imagined spectrum.* The notion made familiar of late that one's sex is assigned rather than discerned at birth is an accommodation to the agenda of gender fluidity. When an obstetrician delivers an infant and looks between the child's legs, sex is being identified (i.e., detected, recognized, discovered) – not assigned (i.e., allocated, attributed, imputed).

Abigail Favale has pointed to the relationship between language and reality found in the Genesis account. In the wide-angle account of creation in Genesis 1, God "uses language to create the cosmos *ex nihilo*: he draws order and being out of nothingness." Then, when the zoomed-in picture of Genesis 2 focuses more tightly on the human creature (Heb, *ha-adam*) who is in God's image as both male and female, we see how "the man uses language to name what God creates. Divine speech makes reality; human speech identifies reality."[19]

Greek philosophy may have tolerated and fostered in places an understanding of human sexuality along a spectrum of beauty and desire – whether focused on male or female form, but the biblical story is different. The body is neither a prison to escape nor

---

[19] Abigail Favale, *The Genesis of Gender: A Christian Theory* (San Francisco: Ignatius Press, 2022), 42.

malleable as to sexual taxonomy and function but is, instead, the locus of God's creative genius.

The understanding of language portrayed in Genesis contrasts starkly with the view that dominates contemporary debates about gender. Most gender theories hold that what we think of as "reality" is a linguistic and social construction. Our use of the words "woman" and "man," so this theory goes, creates the illusion that sex is a binary.... In this divinely revealed origin story, our language does not project meaning onto things. Rather, meaning intrinsically exists in what God creates.... We are unities of body and spirit; our bodies are an integral part of our identity that connect us to the created order and serve as a bridge between our inmost being and the outer world, and a sacramental sign of the hidden mystery of God.[20]

In the Genesis creation story, Adam gave names to all the animals. "But for Adam no suitable helper was found" (Gen 2:20). Each of the animals was a "living creature."[21] But not one of them was "in the image of God" – an expression that speaks to the distinctive nature of humans and our unique relationship to the Creator. So, from part of the man's own body, a woman was created to be a "suitable helper" for the man. The expression "suitable helper" (Heb, *ēzer kenegdo*) occurs only twice in all the Bible at Genesis 2:18b and 2:20b. The language of the text makes it clear that the woman is not to be treated as a slave or some mere assistant to the man. Women are full partners[22] with men as God's image-bearers and fellow-stewards of the Deity's good creation.

---

[20] Ibid., 43.
[21] "Living creature" (NIV, NRSVue) is the Hebrew (*nephesh chayyah*) description in Genesis of sea creatures (1:21), mammals (1:24), and the total collection of animal life (2:19). A human being is also a "living creature" (2:7) – with the distinction of being made also "in the image of God." To be human, therefore, is not to be a body that *has* a soul. It is to be an animate being who bears a unique likeness to and mission from God to bear his image into the created world and to serve God by managing his creation wisely and lovingly.
[22] The Hebrew term *ēzer* is found a total of 21 times in the Old Testament. In 14 of those instances, Yahweh himself is the "helper" or "rescuer" in view (Cf. Ex 18:4; Psa 33:20; 121:1-2). The word does not indicate a slave, servant, or assistant. The woman and man *both* are in God's image – not the man in God's image and the woman in Adam's.

In one of the few times where a Hebrew wordplay survives translation, the special relationship of the original male and female comes through here in English. "The man said, 'This is now bone of my bones and flesh of my flesh; she shall be called "woman," (Heb, *ishah*) for she was taken out of man (Heb, *ish*)'" (Gen 2:24). In Eve's bodily presence, Adam saw *image-of-God sameness* with his own flesh-and-bones body. At the same time, the *gendered difference* from himself was immediately discerned as essential to God's purpose for humans. Female and male were paired now for the purpose of helping or rescuing Adam.

It was not good for the man to be "alone," for, while unaccompanied, a male – or an all-male species of humanity – could never fulfill the original human mission: "Be fruitful and increase in number; fill the earth and subdue it" (Gen 1:28). It had always been the divine plan for human beings to live and function as all "living creatures" do – reproducing and training their young. In addition, humans have the distinctive responsibility to bear God's image into his creation and to rule it wisely and responsibly. Only with a female counterpart and suitable helper could that mission be achieved. "That is why a *man* leaves his father and mother and is united to his *wife*, and they become one flesh" (Gen 2:24). That this male-with-female pairing and partnership is presented as the norm for humankind is clear from the wide-angle language of Genesis 1:27, where the plural pronoun "them" is used twice and then defined as "male *and* female" – as well as from the more detailed account of Genesis 2:18-24.

As two embodied persons in the image of their Creator, Adam and Eve were both designed and destined to become "one flesh" (Gen 2:24b). This is not euphemistic sensitivity but a biblical comment on the depth of commitment involved between two embodied souls. The union of a woman and man in marital sex is so complete that they can be thought of as being not two separate bodies but one.

There is certainly nothing negative toward human sexual expression in these opening lines from the Bible. The nakedness (i.e., total vulnerability) of the man and woman to each other in their sexual natures was hardly a source of shame. It was joyous and celebratory – as that described poetically in the Song of Solomon.

Same-sex intercourse negates the procreative design of human sexuality. It seeks to satisfy the innate desire for bonding within love through a means other than the one established in the divinely created order. The God who loves to create life has created all living things with the power to create still more life. Plants, animals, humans in God's image – everything that lives is given the power to produce life. In the intimacy of married love, the human is empowered to fulfill the original mission given to "be fruitful and increase in number" (Gen 1:28). It is obvious to the point of being trite to say that same-sex intimacy cannot comply with that mission.

In the romantic spirit and language of our time, we are likely to read the "aloneness" of the first male in the Genesis story as "loneliness." We certainly cannot say that Adam did not have the emotional sense we call loneliness, but we can say the text doesn't attribute that feeling to him. That Adam was "alone" was "not good" (Gen 2:18) because he could not comply with the charge to bring new life after his kind into the garden without Eve. Vines is mistaken to claim that "the account of Eve's creation doesn't emphasize Adam's need to procreate. It emphasizes instead his need for relationship."[23] Without being frivolous, perhaps we should be thankful Adam didn't get distracted by a "relationship" with a dog, cat, or other animal that so many people today call their "family" or "baby" – thus eliminating the need for a *differentiated* human.

The purported reasoning that relationship rather than procreation was primary to the creation of Eve doesn't work. Would

---

[23] Vines, *God and the Gay Christian*, 45.

a relationally bonded male have eliminated the "aloneness" of this story? No, but it would have guaranteed the end of the human line. For that matter, does male-female marriage resolve emotional "loneliness" that Vines sees as the real issue for Adam? Many married people I have counseled speak of the "loneliness" they feel in their relationship. If relational bonding is the issue, does that not justify that lonely person to seek a meaningful relationship with someone else? This is the very rationalization offered by countless men and women for their adulterous affairs.

The moral truth is that both same-sex unions *per se* and the breaking of an opposite-sex marital covenant are wrong not simply because they transgress a command but because both violate the divine will as expressed in creation itself. It is that disruption of the created order that generates the biblical prohibitions we will explore in later sections of this book. These banned behaviors are thus universal and transcultural. They are neither limited to a particular time and place nor are they generated from some Bible writer's bigotry – or the bigotry of that author's non-affirming interpreter. They are rooted in the narrative of God's nature and personal activity as recorded in Holy Scripture. They cannot be abandoned without simultaneously giving up the notion that Scripture is to be taken seriously as the written guide to Christian faith.

I am convinced that many single people I have known, befriended, and watched grow to maturity as Christians were never looking for sex. They were looking for the intimacy of human friendship. In their individual cases, their need was not to reproduce but to flourish as persons in the kingdom of God. They have served as physicians, school teachers, staff persons for churches, missionaries, mayors, school board members, and in countless other positions without feeling cheated or punished. On the other hand, I am equally certain that I have known many single, divorced, and widowed persons who have swallowed the modern belief that their fulfillment as persons depended on having a sexual partner. In the lives of these people, occasional successes in beginning a relationship based on sex that morphed into love are massively outnumbered by failed involvements that have left broken hearts, single-parent children, angry adults, and weakened or abandoned spiritual lives in their wake.

What of a Sex-Gender Distinction?

Biblically and scientifically, humans exist as either male or female. To say that sex is binary is simply to say that there are two and only two options. In the rare medical condition known as "intersex," there is a genital ambiguity or genetic variance – but not a "third" sex. Whatever variation may occur in the 0.018% of the human population that is intersex raises legitimate questions of medical care and Christian compassion relative to their bodies. That variation does not invalidate or cast doubt on the unquestionable nature of the 99.982% whose binary status establishes the norm.[24]

While the modern term "gender" is often used to indicate the self-perception of a person of either sex toward that person's comfort with gender expectations (e.g., macho behaviors for males or feminine social requirements for females) or acting against them (e.g., female auto mechanics or male kindergarten teachers), gender variance does not redefine one's sex. Furthermore, whether in rigid Muslim cultures where morality police force females to cover their hair in public or in rigid Christian cults that do the same thing, the gender requirements are enforced on the basis

---

[24] The claim is frequently made by revisionists that the frequency of intersex persons is in the range of 1.7% of the population. It stems from a paper authored by Brown University's Anne Fausto-Sterling, "The Five Sexes," *The Sciences* (March/April 1993): 20-25. The National Institutes of Health, along with a number of researchers and clinicians, have demonstrated the misleading nature of her claim. Abstract of "How Common Is Intersex? A Response to Anne Fausto-Sterling," *Journal of Sex Research* 39 (Aug 2002): 174-178. Cf. Sax, *Why Gender Matters*, 2nd ed. (New York: Random House, 2017). The actual variance is 0.018%.

of sex. In both cases, sex is presumed to dictate gender; birth identity opens or closes doors of what those cultures deem to be gender appropriate. The relationship of sex to gender is therefore tangential, and one may legitimately question both the sex-gender expectations that a given society imposes and the notion of fluid gender-sex identities.

In other words, Malala Yousafzai should not be denied education or be shot by the Taliban for challenging a *gender-limited role* because of her *sex-defined identity* as female. The idea that a woman's testimony in court should count for only half that of a man's or that a female cannot open a bank account without a male's permission is not simply unfair but immoral. At the same time, one's *male-female genetic identity* is not subject to *self-alteration based on personal choice* that is rooted in sexual desire or attraction.

Stated another way, cultural options that our contemporary vocabulary assigns to the category of "gender" have shifted along a spectrum of opportunity and recognition of personal ability. There are still only two identifiable categories of "sex" – male and female – which may either conform, challenge, or be indifferent to those changes. *Gender roles* have been fluid enough to undergo modification, while the fixed *sexual taxonomy* of two and only two sexes has remained immutable.

Gender Dysphoria

Parents, educators, psychologists, and other ethically sensitive persons express legitimate concern over what is called *gender dysphoria*. Defined as an individual's sense of psychic distress that his or her "birth-assigned sex" differs from her or his "authentic gender identity," gender dysphoria has given rise to some very manipulative claims out of the LGBTQ+ community and its supporters and, as well, to a number of irresponsible "therapies" by the mental health and traditional medical communities.

An example of the manipulative-claim scenario is the first chapter of Matthew Vines' book and the opening point of the Reformation Project's website. The essential claim is that persons who maintain a traditional (i.e., non-affirming) posture on same-sex behaviors "contribute to serious harm in LGBTQ people's lives."[25] In political settings, left-wing activists describe puberty blockers, sex-transition counseling, cross-sex hormone therapy, and surgery as "lifesaving" and warn of suicides among transgender children if these services are not provided to all comers. From the right-wing partisans, both legitimate concerns and demeaning rhetoric toward trans young people as "mutants" and their enablers as "demons" can be heard.

Sensible voices have avoided these extreme posturings and claims. Even such non-conservative publications as the *Washington Post* and *New York Times* have carried nuanced reports that raise serious concerns over the rush to embrace "affirmative care" by many in the American mental health and medical communities. An article in *The Atlantic* that summarizes much of the ongoing exchange points out that childhood gender dysphoria resolves itself in approximately 80% of cases and warns against allowing "groupthink" to replace good evidence.[26] The same article points out that researchers and clinicians in countries who were among the first to adopt transition therapies – England, France, Norway, Sweden, Finland – are slowing rather than accelerating their programs because of the potential for long-term harmful effects. Sweden's National Board of Health and Welfare is quoted that

---

[25] "Experience of sound Christian teaching should show good fruit, not bad fruit," *The Reformation* Project, https://reformationproject.org/case/good-vs-bad-fruit.
[26] Helen Lewis, "The Only Way out of the Child-Gender Culture War," *The Atlantic*, May 4, 2023, https://www.theatlantic.com/ideas/archive/2023/05/texas-puberty-blockers-gender-care-transgender-rights/673941.

risks from puberty blockers and cross-sex hormones "currently outweigh the possible benefits" of their use.

An article in the *New York Times*[27] reports its review of scientific papers and interviews with more than 50 physicians and academics around the world and gives this warning about puberty blockers: "The drugs suppress estrogen and testosterone, hormones that help develop the reproductive system but also affect the bones, the brain and other parts of the body." While citing cases where both professionals and patients affirm what they have done, the piece also documents the "false positives" and de-transitioning of others. One female who halted her medical transitioning at 18 to resume her biological identity "is left with a voice that sounds like a man's and other enduring physical changes." Are the dangers here not obvious? Do 11-year-olds or 14-year-olds – much less those even younger – know whether they want to be math teachers or astronauts? Live in California or North Carolina? Care for a puppy or not? Yet upon their expressed desire to change sex (a biological impossibility), parents, counselors, physicians, and courts insist their wishes be honored? Strange. Very strange indeed.

Gender dysphoria is real, and what horrendous suffering it must cause to feel an internal tension between one's given biological sex and one's social pull to different gender functions. While condemning all forms of injustice and violence toward such persons, the Christian path – which typically is countercultural in almost every aspect – calls for accepting the fixed gift of one's biological identity and seeking help with the mental, emotional, and spiritual aspects of healing (or, in many cases, simply growing through) a perceived mismatch of gender function.

---

[27] Megan Twohey and Christina Jewett, "They Paused Puberty, but Is There a Cost?", *New York Times*, Nov 14, 2022, https://www.nytimes.com/2022/11/14/health/puberty-blockers-transgender.html.

The best evidence is that most people who experience gender dysphoria will work through its minor vestiges as they mature through life experience. For those whose situation is severe and in need of help, a spiritual guide or professional therapist will be helpful when assisting persons to align their subjective inner state with their biological status and injurious to spiritual health by working in the opposite direction.

To say the least, the frequently repeated claim that Christian failure to adopt an affirming view of same-sex relationships is dangerous and produces suicidal behavior is open to challenge. While it *is* true that suicide attempts are significantly higher in the LGBTQ+ community than in the general population, suicide is seldom traceable to a single cause. A person taking his own life generally is dealing with multiple mental-health issues. A study published in the *Archives of Sexual Behavior* shows the suicide rate among adolescent persons diagnosed with gender dysphoria in relation to young people with other mental health diagnoses is not significantly different between the two groups.[28]

What is certain about Vines' use of Jesus' metaphor about a tree and its fruit is that he has misinterpreted and misapplied the point of Matthew 7:15-20. In the Sermon on the Mount, the "bad fruit" of certain prophets is their lifestyle that contradicts and undermines their teaching. If Jesus rebuked behavior criticisms that might make someone feel bad, stop going to church, or consider suicide, would that not make Vines culpable for rebuking adultery, prostitution, and rape? What would it say about Jesus' scathing rebuke of the

---

[28] Kenneth J. Zucker, "Adolescents with Gender Dysphoria: Reflections on Some Contemporary Clinical and Research Issues," *Archives of Sexual Behavior* (July 2019), https://genderchallenge.no/onewebmedia/Zucker2019_Article_AdolescentsWithGenderDysphoria.pdf. Also, a Scandinavian study available at https://pubmed.ncbi.nlm.nih.gov/31762394 concluded: "Medical gender reassignment is not enough to improve functioning and relieve psychiatric comorbidities among adolescents with gender dysphoria. Appropriate interventions are warranted for psychiatric comorbidities and problems in adolescent development."

Pharisees or his instruction that the woman caught in adultery should "leave your life of sin"?

Conclusion

Finally, if – as this chapter has claimed – the proper place for human sexual relationships traces to the Garden of Eden and affirms only covenantal marriage between one man and one woman for life, what of single people? Are single, divorced, or widowed persons somehow "unfinished" or "incomplete" until they can find a partner for marriage? Nothing of that sort follows from the Bible's opening narrative about male-female marriage.

The Genesis story is the account of how our *collective humanity* – regardless of the male or female, single or married state of any individual – works to reach its assigned goal. It is not a description of what each individual must attain to be personally whole.

Sadly, some Christian teachers and writers have not only left the impression but have explicitly said that males and females are somehow "incomplete" until they find a marital partner. Absurd! Otherwise, the elderly prophet Anna (who had been a widow for decades, cf. Luke 2:36-37a), eunuchs (whether born eunuchs or surgically castrated, cf. Matt 19:12), or never-married virgins at Corinth (cf. 1 Cor 7:25-28) were only "half-finished souls"? The singles group at my church is a cluster of "deficient" people? One of my dearest friends and colleagues in ministry is single and chaste by choice. And, lest we forget, so was Jesus of Nazareth. So was at least one of his apostles, Paul.

In explaining his own choice about being unmarried, Paul said it gave him more freedom and flexibility for travel, teaching, and serving (especially in hard fields of missionary work) than he could have had if responsible for the welfare of a wife and children (vs.32-35; cf. 9:5). The only option some Christian parents seem to offer their children is education, marriage, and grandchildren for them. Why are we reluctant to suggest careers in mission work for our children who are interested in other languages and cultures? Bible translation for our children who excel at language studies? Working – as a single friend of mine who is a nurse practitioner chose to do – on a terribly underserved reservation for Native Americans in New Mexico?

Marriage is not required of any member of the race, but marriage between one woman and one man is the mandatory context for sexual expression by any member of the human race. And that norm goes all the way back to Eden.

Life on Planet Earth would have been so very, very different if the garden had not been spoiled. But, alas, things have gone awry.

2

Questions for Reflection

THINK ABOUT . . .
THE IMPORTANCE OF NARRATIVE
IN THE BIBLICAL MATERIALS

The Bible is not an instruction manual or catalog of rules. It is chock full of various literary genres – poetry and prophecy, laments and letters, prayers and parables, dreams and dialogues. The most common of all is simply narrative. Narratives – not just the laws embedded in them – are authoritative to reveal God, show us how he works, lay out the storyline of redemption, and call human beings into the story. Creation is just such a narrative.

EXPLORE . . .
MATTHEW 19:1-9

This block of text shows how the one who has ultimate spiritual authority saw Scripture function for his disciples. When presented with a question about marriage and divorce, he pointed them to the creation narrative as precedent for how marriages are supposed to work and as justification for the anti-divorce laws designed to protect it. Does this teach us anything about the importance of that same narrative for all one-flesh relationships?

Practice . . .
Life within the narrative of Eden

For centuries, the stories of creation, the Garden of Eden, and the one-flesh union of Adam and Eve have been viewed as an ideal story of human life. Humans lived without shame in the presence of and shared intimacy with their Creator. Since the fall, God has been calling us back to that life – not excusing the harm sin did to it.

1. Revisionist writers typically see these ideal traits in Genesis 1-2 and Jesus' use of that narrative: spousal bonding, sexual union, monogamy, fidelity, and mutual support. Explain how the story suggests them.

2. The same writers do *not* see sex/gender diversity as relevant to the story. Why would it be extraneous?

3. Reflect on what this chapter says about embodied personhood. Why are both *commonality* and *difference* crucial to the creation story?

4. In the biblical story of creation, what do you understand "It is not good for the man to be alone" to mean?

5. Comment on gender dysphoria and how it is being responded to in our culture.

6. What is your most important takeaway from Chapter Two?

Chapter 3 offers a historical perspective on the biblical world into which Jesus came and in which the apostles preached the story of salvation in him. Because it is so important to put their statements and writings into their original context, perhaps this quotation from Scot McKnight will begin painting a picture of the sexual lives of the larger Roman Empire for you.

Studies of the sexual lives of Roman (or Greek) men reveal a typical pattern: males had "procreational" sex with their wives, with whom they shared a home, children, and a family life, and had "recreational" sex with others. . . .

In their sexual recreations, some husbands participated in sex with women while some of these husbands also engaged in same-sex relations on the side. Paul is describing this sort of relationship in 1 Corinthians 6:9, which reads "men who have sex with men" (NIV), but the explanatory footnote clarifies that the words "refer to the passive and active participants." . . . When we ask, "Who were those who engaged in same-sex relations in Paul's day?" we are then to think mostly of married males engaging in same-sex relations recreationally. Since committed same-sex relations were known in the Roman world, 1 Corinthians 6:9-11 could be describing faithful same-sex couples, but this is less likely than a Roman husband's recreational sex with other men.

Lesbianism existed but was not nearly as pervasive as same-sex relations among males. Lucian, writing in the century after the apostle Paul, says, "They say there are women like that in Lesbos, masculine-looking, but they don't want to give it up for men. Instead, they consort with women, just like men."

Scot McKnight, *A Fellowship of Differents*
(Grand Rapids: Zondervan, 2014), 124-125.

*The past is a foreign country:
they do things differently there.*

−L.P. Hartley

3

A World in Rebellion

When I began serious Bible study as a young adult, my impression was that the most difficult part of that process would be language mastery. As with so many things about those early days of trying to be a resolute and fair-minded reader of the Bible, I was mistaken and have had to adjust my thinking over time. That comment is not meant to sell the study of Hebrew and Greek short, mind you, but to place them in perspective. I have come to believe that the most critical part of Bible study is *historical context*.

As the Hartley quote at the top of this page puts it, the past really is a "foreign country." What an insightful metaphor. Whether the issue is government, marriage, science, or perhaps even geography, things as we experience them today are not what my American parents or our European ancestors experienced. For example, today's university-educated American female cannot imagine the world into which my mother was born. Women could not vote. Much less could they hold high public office, attend medical school, or practice law. In my mother's case relative to science, she had grown up in a world without antibiotics and must have been terribly concerned when a doctor diagnosed her months-old youngest child with pneumonia early in 1946. But he had recently gained access to a "wonder drug" developed at lightning speed during World War II called penicillin and got my parents' permission to administer it to me. They both were convinced it saved my life.

Even geography has changed radically since the year I was first given penicillin. There is a curiosity piece I still have from my parents' home that proves it. *Hammond's Superior Atlas and Gazetteer of the World,* copyrighted in 1946 by the Publishers Guild of New York, has not only countries identified that no longer exist and demographic data that is useless for current purposes but also topographical maps that are no longer accurate.

Studying the world of only a century ago is a real challenge. They were "doing things differently there." The things we take for granted were not part of their experience. So, if we naively think of their world in terms of ours, the assumptions we carry from our experience into theirs will be as disorienting as your being set down in a foreign country where you do not know anyone, cannot speak the language of the people, and have no means of contact with the world to which you belong and in which you know how to function.

What, then, is the importance of such disciplines as history, archaeology, art, and foreign language to Bible study? Languages such as Hebrew, Aramaic, Greek, and Latin are unquestionably important to careful reading of the sacred texts. But the value of knowing those languages is for the sake of giving us access into the larger concern of the total historical setting from which the Old and New Testaments emerged. What world powers were stamping their varied cultures and standards on people in the day of Moses, Amos, or Peter? What rights or limitations were presumed for women such as Deborah, Mary, or Phoebe? How did marriage and family life work? What behaviors were approved in Assyrian or Greco-Roman times that were offensive and condemned in the Jewish culture(s) embedded in them?

If we are insensitive to the historical setting of biblical events and texts, we will be likely to misread them. But how difficult will it be to get reliable information and to construct a clear picture of those ancient times? By what standards should we evaluate the competing interpretations offered by scholars? And how can we guard against seeing what we want to see in order to support a present practice for which we are seeking historical precedent?

The most challenging part of Bible study is to read our ancient texts in light of the best-evidenced background for the persons, events, and literary forms found in its pages. Thus, for our study of the sexual standards and behaviors in Scripture, we have to do some digging into history before opening a biblical text and reading it either in an intellectual vacuum or from the framework of our own twenty-first century position in history.

Sex Apart from Male-Female Marriage

From Eden and beyond in the biblical documents, we discover a creature *brought into being by the Creator's will* who henceforth will be *permitted to express the creature's will.* There will be no coercion or forced compliance. The larger Earth environment will not always be tended with the foresight and care the Creator's handiwork deserves. The image of God stamped on the males and females commissioned to bear his image responsibly will too often be marred and defaced by sin. But it was always the loving intention of the Creator to give each of us the personal choice between following his will and choosing to reject it for our own. Lacking that freedom, we would hardly be "living creatures" – much less humans in the divine image – but programmed robots.

Because the creature chose to defy the Creator's good purpose and will, the Bible quickly becomes the redemptive story of God's loving pursuit of his wayward human creatures. It is not primarily concerned with sexual matters and certainly does not supply a detailed account of human sexual history. Yet, just as food, drink, and creative work give humans pleasure and carry the risk of becoming obsessions, the same thing appears to have happened with sex. Furthermore, within the varied cultures of Egypt, Persia, or Rome – to name only three of several more – what cultural expectations surrounded the choices open to the biblical characters? Were God's chosen people allowed to live by the mores of time and place? Or were they held accountable to a different standard?

Outside its proper place in a loving and committed bond between one man and one woman, sexual experience quickly becomes the means to dehumanize and exploit others. Slavery, prostitution, rape as a weapon of war, pornography, pederasty, pedophilia – all these are clear cases of dehumanization that see some people being used as instruments for the satisfaction of others' lust – whether that "lust" is for sex, money, or power. And history gives us clear indications of that fact. Satan also uses the obvious pleasure associated with sexual intercourse to seduce both single and married persons into relationships that often incur guilt and negative personal consequences – as well as causing them to sin and jeopardize their relationship with God.

The biblical counsel is constant in calling people to live in holiness before God. "As obedient children, do not conform to the evil desire you had when you lived in ignorance. But just as he who called you is holy, so be holy in all you do; for it is written: 'Be holy, because I am holy'" (1 Pet 1:15-16; cf. Lev 19:1-2).

The claim so often repeated by affirming writers about ancient cultures having nothing that corresponded to the modern-day social acceptance of committed same-sex relationships is seriously mistaken. While male-male and female-female sexual couplings have been in the minority and were sometimes kept hidden because of public disapproval in certain cultures, there have been numerous successful attempts before our own time to "normalize" and cultivate public tolerance for them. In the chart at the end of this chapter, I have identified only a few of the well-documented cases of LGBTQ+ activities from the Greco-Roman period. From the eighth century B.C. into the third Christian century, these are instances of public figures, widely circulated religious myths or poetic pieces, and celebrated public figures. One or more – and certainly all of them collectively – show conclusively that this claim already cited in Chapter Two is false: "There are no ancient examples of lifelong, monogamous same-sex relationships between social equals, and certainly none that have societal support."

The only endorsed and safeguarded paradigm for sexual coupling to which we can point in the Bible is male-with-female marriage lived in committed, faithful, and loving partnership. This is the model that we saw emerge from Eden. For this relationship, there was no shame. When Adam and Eve chose to sin against their Creator and were expelled from their original ideal setting, the only thing it seems they were able to bring with them was their relationship. God had joined them. Various shifting sands of cultural movements would threaten that relationship. But the prophets of God – including the Incarnate Messiah for whose coming they had longed – would consistently call them away from the retooled versions of marriage they encountered to what they had known "from the beginning."

EXAMPLES OF SAME-SEX UNIONS IN ANTIQUITY

Every society educates its children about what it considers to be acceptable behavior through poems, religious narratives, and stories of its cultural heroes. These accounts – in the tradition of Aesop's fables, *McGuffey's Readers*, Pinocchio, and Bible stories – offer early-life impressions of behaviors that are appropriate for imitation. In his *Republic*, the philosopher Plato famously warned against allowing unworthy stories of the Greek gods "warring, fighting, or plotting against one another" to circulate in Athens, lest children get the wrong ideas about what constitutes acceptable behavior.

In light of Plato's warning, it is interesting that his dialogue named the *Symposium* features a man named Pausanias who makes a distinction between two types of love. The first he calls "Common Aphrodite's Love"; it is the passion of orgasmic ecstasy, is common to those who take either male or female partners, and "all they care about is completing the sexual act."[29] By contrast, he offers "Love of Heavenly Aphrodite," which is superior; it is attracted to males rather than females, "prefers older ones whose cheeks are showing the first traces of a beard" – a sign that they have begun to form minds of their own – and forms a lasting bond with their partners. "I am convinced that a man who falls in love with a young man of this age is generally prepared to share everything with the one he loves," insists Pausanias, "he is eager, in fact, to spend the rest of his own life with him."[30] To spend the rest of his life with him? For an older man to court a younger man and then have that relationship evolve into a loving commitment for life sounds like the more common experience of how male-female courtship and marriage worked in the same historical period.

Two things are especially significant here. First, the Athens of Plato's day is known for its approval of pederasty among elite citizens – the very public and approved relationship between an older mentor and an adolescent male he would tutor into civic life and a career. The recommendation in the *Symposium* is that a man's love for an older male that lasts a lifetime is superior to some brief and possibly exploitative liaison. Second, in direct contradiction to the claim that no ancient examples of lifelong, monogamous same-sex relationships between social equals and with societal support can be found, two

---

[29] Plato, *Symposium* 181b.
[30] Plato, *Symposium* 181d.

historical personages of Athens featured in this dialogue – Pausanias and his poet-lover Agathon – had been in a committed same-sex relationship for over 30 years when the dialogue was written.

Not long after Plato wrote his *Symposium*, the Greek city-state of Thebes formed a fighting force of 300 same-sex warriors to defend against Sparta. Thebes was the principal Greek city-state of Boeotia in Central Greece. Classics professor James Romm, who wrote the definitive book on *The Sacred Band*,[31] points to the special support given to male unions there. "It's the first we hear, in any Greek city," notes Romm, "of a legislative program designed to encourage same-sex pair bonding."[32] Xenophon of Athens wrote in the fourth century B.C. of Boeotian male partners who lived as "yoke-mates" – language used in that period of male-female married couples. Romm also cites the practice of male couples coming to a special site in Thebes to pledge their vows of love and fidelity as mates for life.

The story of the infantry regiment from Thebes that consisted of 150 adult male couples has received a bit of special notice in the past few years. Described by their fellow-Boeotian Plutarch in his *Parallel Lives*, the fighting corps was formed in 378 B.C. in response to the aggressive behavior of Sparta against Thebes. Some Plato scholars believe its organization was likely influenced by a comment in the *Symposium* that an army of lovers would be near-invincible because no man would want his lover to see him turn and flee from danger.[33] Plutarch attributed the particular bravery and effectiveness of the Band in its various military exploits to the same motivation. At any rate, the Band was formed and distinguished itself seven years later when the Theban military defeated the Spartans in pitched battle.

---

[31] James Romm, *The Sacred Band: Three Hundred Theban Lovers and the Last Days of Greek Freedom* (New York: Scribner, 2021).
[32] James Romm, "The Legacy of Same-Sex Love in Ancient Thebes," *History News Network*, June 6, 2021, https://historynewsnetwork.org/article/180453.
[33] Plato, *Symposium* 178a-180b.

Until the nineteenth century, the story of the so-called Sacred Band as related by Plutarch was questioned by some historians. Specific to our point of committed same-sex love, Romm notes that the doubters "suggested the erotic principle described in the *Lives* was only a fiction." We know today that the Theban soldiers were wiped out by the forces of Philip of Macedon, the father of Alexander the Great, at the Battle of Chaeronea in 338 B.C.

> The mass grave of the Band was uncovered at Chaeronea, the spot where they fell in battle, and sketches were made of their remains by Panagiotis Stamatakis, the chief excavator. These sketches, uncovered by Greek archivists only in the past few years, reveal that pairs of corpses were interred with arms linked – dramatic confirmation of Plutarch's account.[34]

Moving from Greece to the Roman Empire, the approving attitude toward pederasty among the ruling elites changed somewhat, but the practice of same-sex relationships among consenting adults did not. Perhaps more typically between males of the same age than between older and younger men,[35] these relationships are documented by some of Rome's most prolific and widely read literary figures. The poet Martial (*ca.*40-*ca.*103) seems to have become particularly popular among the city's literate citizens by writing on such subjects as the gluttony, ambition, furniture, food, and the sex lives of his contemporaries. In one poem, he relates that a "bearded Callistratus as a bride wedded the brawny

---

[34] Romm, "Legacy."

[35] We tend to forget that ancient cultures – and many of our own time – generally expected there to be a considerable age gap between a suitor and his mate. In marriages arranged between families, the concern would be that the pursuing partner would be older, established in his work, and able to support the younger party. This was true in the Jewish community of the first century and likely explains why a young Mary was still alive at her son's death in AD 30, whereas the absent Joseph is presumed to have died. In same-sex arrangements, the age gap surely varied as well. So the gap in age between two males in the Roman Period no more made their relationship pederastic in their time and place than the age gap between an adult groom and his considerably younger bride would have made theirs a case of child molestation.

Afer in the usual form as when a virgin weds a husband."³⁶ What he is describing is hardly a pederastic arrangement.

Julius Caesar (100-44 B.C.), Emperor Galba (3 B.C.–A.D.69), Nero (37-68), the famously transgender adult males of the Cult of Cybele (200 B.C.-A.D. 200), the male-male and female-female erotica of Pompeii (destroyed in A.D. 79) – all these very public figures and details from the Roman Empire, along with the continued stories of the Greco-Roman gods and legendary heroes, make it practically impossible for Jesus, Peter, and Paul to have been unaware of same-sex alternatives to traditional marriage in their lifetimes.

There really is nothing new about same-sex relationships – whether as anonymous one-night stands, romantic liaisons with one or more persons over time, civil unions, or "marriages." What will be clear from the Old and New Testament materials to be examined in the next two chapters is that *there is no form of same-sex coupling to which God has given approval in Holy Scripture.*

HISTORIANS AND CLASSICISTS ON THE SUBJECT

The late John Boswell, a Yale history professor and himself gay and a strong advocate of same-sex unions, commented that Roman same-sex relationships have been less studied than those of Greek culture. However, as the somewhat formal and institutionalized norms of Athens gave way to what is generally seen to be a "riotous and promiscuous sexuality" of Rome, he insists that "there were also many same-sex couples in the Roman world who lived together permanently, forming unions neither more nor less exclusive than those of the heterosexual couples around them."³⁷ To support his view, he proceeds to list a number of documented instances of same-sex couples – several of which provide evidence of the use of the term "marriage" of their relationship.

---

³⁶ Martial, *Epigrams* 12.42.
³⁷ John Boswell, *Same-Sex Unions in Premodern Europe* (New York: Villard Books, 1994), 65.

The first instance Boswell offers is found in the writings of Cicero (106-43 B.C.) and the second – which he terms "the most famous romantic couple in imperial Rome" – is from the second Christian century. Thus, from a century before Jesus and Paul to a century after their deaths, adult sexual coupling existed in the New Testament world.

Since Boswell's book, the published research of classicists such as Kyle Harper of the University of Oklahoma has expanded our knowledge of how gay persons lived in the Roman Empire and the literary description – both biblical and non-biblical – of those relationships. In his book that received the 2014 Award for Excellence from the American Academy of Religion, Harper summarizes the current status of work on Roman sexual culture by historians and classicists. It shows conclusively that pederasty was *not* the only model of same-sex relationship known in antiquity and that long-term, committed, authentically caring, and mutually supportive same-sex relationships unquestionably existed in New Testament times.

> It scarcely needs saying that same-sex marriages between women, or men, had no standing or consequence in public law, but that fact hardly diminishes the extraordinary testimony we do have for durable forms of same-sex companionship. In a peaceful and prosperous society, amid a highly urbanized and remarkably interconnected empire where marriage was valorized as an institution of the greatest moral and emotional fulfillment, same-sex pairs openly claimed, and ritually enacted, their own conjugal rights.
>
> It is beyond our ken to say how people truly behaved in any period of history. But at the very least it is time to lay to rest the bizarre notion, which is still sometimes expressed, that same-sex eros was, materially and ideologically, on the wane by the second century. . . . Indeed, same-sex eros was of greater interest to the Latin writers on either side of AD 100 than ever before; and as the Greek sources come to preponderance in the second century, there is no sign of abatement.[38]

---

[38] Kyle Harper, *From Shame to Sin: The Christian Transformation of Sexual Morality in Late Antiquity* (Cambridge, MA: Harvard University Press, 2013), 36.

The Biblical Thesis for This Study

Based on a straightforward reading of the literature, it is impossible to put together an affirmative case that either Scripture or church history shows the earliest Christians giving their approval to same-sex relationships. Neither do the facts support the claim that such relationships in antiquity were only exploitative and thus quite different from what is possible today. Put most simply and directly, the biblical prohibitions of same-sex activity and relationships cannot be dismissed as referring to something that was quite unlike today's consensual, long-term, and committed same-sex partnerships.

I emphasize again, however, that the purpose of this study is not negative. Its focus will not be on a handful of texts that caricature one type of sexual behavior as sinful above all others. Those texts, often lumped under the heading "clobber texts" – which is, of course, merely a negative rhetorical device – are not central to the biblical text. They are incidental and secondary to the affirmation and protection the Bible offers one-man, one-woman marriage. They are boundary markers to safeguard healthy sexual intimacy. Instead, my *positive goal* is to affirm the one righteous context in which God has created sex to function and in which he will bless it. Here is the most straightforward statement I could imagine to summarize my thesis . . .

> Marriage should be honored by all,
> and the marriage bed kept pure,
> for God will judge the adulterer and
> all the sexually immoral.
>
> *(Hebrews 13:4)*

In its biblical design, *marriage* is the covenant bond between one male and one female who have come together to participate in the divine mission of honoring God by creating new life and providing spiritual encouragement and social connectedness to all its members. Marriage is designed to foster the divine purpose of bringing the reign of God to Earth, as it already exists in Heaven.

Thus, it is imperative that *the marriage bed be kept pure* of sin. Until a man and woman are married, the biblical word used of any sexual intercourse between them is *fornication*. For anyone who already is married to have sex with a third party violates his or her covenant promise of exclusive devotion. He or she thereby becomes an *adulterer* (i.e., covenant-breaker).

At various points in the pages that follow, persons who are single will be challenged to be sexually chaste. Celibacy as a lifetime commitment is for a relative few people, but sexual chastity is the calling of God to all. Whether you plan to marry or not, your body belongs to God, is a temple of the Holy Spirit, and was never meant for immorality but for Christ's service. *Read 1 Cor 6:12-20.*

If you are married, you will be challenged to enrich or, if necessary, heal your relationship. Your physical, emotional, and spiritual welfare – and that of your mate – is tied directly to your willingness to love unselfishly as you have been loved by God. Jesus' model of faithful love for his church reminds you to live with your wife or husband in absolute fidelity. *Read Ephesians 5:21-33.*

If you are widowed, divorced, or single (whether by choice or circumstance), cultivate Christian friendships, find a community of believers (i.e., a Christ-honoring church) to be extended family in your life, and use your life circumstance to serve Christ and the church in ways you might not be able as a married person. If God brings someone into your life as a potential marriage partner, pray and discern his or her love for Christ above all else. The surest seal of human love in godly marriage is to be – and to be with – someone who loves Jesus even more than his or her mate. *Read Colossians 3:1-17.*

Whatever your life situation, live to honor God in all things and find strength for each day from the Spirit of God. The Spirit will orient you to the love of God and neighbor that fulfills the great commandments given by Jesus. That same surrender will make the things that erode spiritual health less and less appealing to you. Pray for strength to resist anger, selfishness, pornography, greed – anything that is a special temptation to you. *Read Galatians 5:13-26.*

Finally, if you are reading this with a sense of guilt and heaviness because of your failure to follow God's will, don't lose heart. If the guilt of sin is a heavy weight you still carry, know that God's love, Christ's blood, and the Spirit's presence are able to rescue you. Wash away your sin. Transform your life. *Read 1 Corinthians 6:9-11 and Ephesians 2:1-10.*

CONCLUSION

Because setting the biblical materials in their proper historical context is so crucial, this chapter has focused on some of the literature available to us that proves same-sex unions – not only exploitative ones such as prostitution or rape but voluntary and committed-for-life unions as well – were known in antiquity. To claim that God enfleshed as Jesus of Nazareth or the well-educated Paul were simply "ignorant" of such relationships entails a view of Scripture that simply defies believability. Within the Torah tradition of both Jesus and Paul, both lived at a time when the Jewish attitude toward same-sex unions was uniform.

That uniform teaching of Second Temple Judaism was that same-sex intercourse is outside God's will – regardless of the context (e.g., wartime rape, pedophilia, prostitution, consent, covenant) in which it occurs.

Having made the case in this chapter from a brief survey of historical materials that people in ancient times would have known all these settings and that what we are dealing with today is *not* a new topic, we can proceed to look directly at some of the key materials that address it and express the biblical case against it.

SOME DOCUMENTED REFERENCES TO LGBTQ+ ACTIVITIES IN THE GRECO-ROMAN PERIOD[39]

ca. 730 B.C.	Philolaus & Diocles	Aristotle
	adult male lovers with a lifelong commitment to each other that began as a pederastic relationship	
ca. 400 B.C.	Orestes & Pylades	Greek play by Euripedes
	regarded as models of lifelong adult love in various poems for generations in both Greece and Rome	
ca. 350 B.C.	Boeotian "yoke-mates"	Xenophon
	same-sex unions "sanctioned by the state" / tomb of Iolaus in Thebes became favored site for taking vows	
ca. 371-338 B.C.	The Sacred Band of Thebes	Plutarch
	famous story of 150 same-sex adult partners as defenders of Thebes	
ca. 400-350 B.C.	Pausanias & Agathon	Friends of Plato
	citizens of Athens in committed relationship for more than 30 years	
ca. 335 B.C.	Damon & Pythias	Valerius Maximus
	loyal to each other in the face of accusations of treason by Dionysius I of Syracuse	
200 B.C. – A.D. 200	Cult of Cybele	Multiple sources
	cult that featured transgender and non-binary adult males in various rituals	
3 B.C. – A.D. 69	Galba	Multiple sources
	notorious in his time for what is generally regarded as exclusive preference for males	
A.D. 37-68	Nero & Pythagoras	Multiple sources
	Nero's "second" marriage in which he appears to have adopted female role for himself	
A.D. 79	Pompeii destroyed	Multiple sources
	archaeological remains show various male-male and female-female erotica	
A.D. 76-138	Hadrian & Antinous	Multiple sources
	"most famous romantic couple" in second-century Rome	

---

[39] Documentation for these relationships and information about additional ones is in *Male and Female God Created Them*, 183-244.

3

Questions for Reflection

THINK ABOUT . . .
THE NATURE OF SCRIPTURE AS A HISTORICAL DOCUMENT

Scripture – like its central figure – is both divine and human. Its content is God-breathed and authoritative to every generation and culture. That content has been delivered to us in human language within human history and in the context of specific human cultures. If we are too lazy to use good resources available to us that put biblical texts in their correct contexts, we can miss the crucial content of the message itself.

EXPLORE . . .
LUKE 10:25-37

The Parable of the Good Samaritan is a simple illustration of the importance of reading the Bible in its historical setting and with an appreciation for the cultural nuances in play. What are some of the characters, relationships, terms, and actions in this story that would need explanation for a first-time reader of the Bible to grasp the power of this story? Can you still "get the point"? How do you see this relating to the issues of this book?

PRACTICE . . .
INFORMED INTERPRETATION OF THE BIBLE

1. This chapter addresses ancient *history* and *culture* prior to studying OT/NT texts on sexuality. Why?

2. What is the concept of "holiness" in the Bible?

3. Explain why not only historical characters but also ancient legends and "gods" belong in the chart that documents familiarity with same-sex relationships.

4. Summarize the facts given about Plato's *Symposium*, the Sacred Band of Thebes, and behaviors among Rome's emperors.

5. How plausible is it that same-sex relationships were unknown to Jesus, Paul, and the first-century church?

6. What is your most important takeaway from Chapter Three?

In his book on biblical interpretation, Scot McKnight calls attention to the way many of us read Scripture. It is a good quotation to whet your appetite for what lies ahead in Chapter 4. See what you think about his very serious caution to all of us.

Some people read the Bible as if its passages were Rorschach inkblots. They see what is in their head. In more sophisticated language, they project onto the Bible what they want to see. If you show them enough passages and you get them to talk about them, you will hear what is important to *them*, whether it is in the Bible or not! They might see in the "Jesus inkblot" a Republican or a socialist, because they are Republicans or socialists. Or, they may see in the book of Revelation, a favorite of inkblot readers, a sketch of contemporary international strife. Or, they may have discerned in the inkblot called "Paul" a wonderful pattern for how to run a church, which just happens to be the pastor's next big plan! You get the point – reading the Bible as an inkblot is projecting onto the Bible *our* ideas and *our* desires. . . .

Instead of being swept into the Bible's story, Rorschach thinkers sweep the Bible up into their own story. Instead of being an opportunity for redemption, the Bible becomes an opportunity for narcissism. This is the problem with taking this shortcut: reading the Bible becomes patting ourselves on the back and finding our story in the Bible, instead of finding the Bible's story to be our story. Instead of entering into that story, we manipulate the story so it enters into our story.

Scot McKnight, *The Blue Parakeet: Rethinking How You Read the Bible* (Grand Rapids: Zondervan, 2008), 48-49.

> *The Old Testament is not something that we try to accommodate ourselves to as though it were an alien book, belonging to someone else and ours at second hand. It is our book.*
>
> – Alec Motyer

4

What the Old Testament Says

"Why bother taking up time with what the *Old* Testament has to say about this subject – or any other for that matter – because we live under the *New* Testament?" asks someone. "Wasn't the Old Testament just for the Jews? And isn't the New Testament really 'new' by its embrace of both Jews and non-Jews into a single spiritual family – with a brand-new set of beliefs, values, and standards? Let's just go straight to the part of the Bible that concerns us. There are some stories back there that really make my hair curl! I'd rather not have to deal with the 'angry' God who kept sending out armies to murder and pillage!"

That language would surely startle Jesus, outrage Paul, and has been declared heretical in the early days of Christianity.

It would *startle* Jesus because it directly contradicts his own teaching about the Law and the Prophets – the Jewish way of referring to Israel's canon of Scripture. "Do not think that I have come to abolish the Law or the Prophets," he said in his Sermon on the Mount. "I have not come to abolish them but to fulfill them" (Matt 5:17). His fulfillment mission had to do with bringing to completion the ancient covenant promise that "all peoples on earth" would be blessed through someone from Abraham's lineage (cf. Gen 12:3). Circumcision, dietary laws, animal sacrifice – these cultic separators and types enacted within Israel would then be fulfilled, made irrelevant, and disclaimed as having perpetual relevance. Said positively, in his fulfillment of the Law and the Prophets, Jesus modeled them in perfect righteousness, taught them with perfect insight, and forever established their perfect ethical relevance to the kingdom reign of God on Earth that he was launching.

That the moral strictures of the Law and the Prophets were not abolished or replaced is evident from two facts. First, Jesus said just that – both explicitly and implicitly. *Explicitly*, even as he declared the dietary limitations of the Torah no longer mandatory, he listed the primary ethical violations of the Law of Moses as evils that defile a person. In the same breath by which "Jesus declared all foods clean" to his followers, he listed "sexual immorality, theft, murder, adultery, greed, malice, deceit, lewdness, envy, slander, arrogance and folly" as typical evil deeds that "come from inside and defile a person" (Mark 7:17-23). *Implicitly*, it is clear that he was not setting aside the moral as well as messiah-anticipating predictions and types of our Old Testament by virtue of the fact that his Sermon on the Mount expounds his "I have not come to abolish *them*" with an immediate commentary on six moral teachings of the Torah – murder, adultery, divorce, oath-taking, personal retaliation, and love for neighbor (Matt 5:21-48).

Why would Paul be *outraged* by such a claim? It was after Jesus' fulfillment of the Law and Prophets that he wrote this: "All Scripture is God-breathed and is useful for teaching, rebuking, correcting and training in righteousness" (2 Tim 3:16). It is beyond question that what Paul calls Scripture in this classic text about divine revelation is our Old Testament. In the verse immediately prior, he has celebrated "how from infancy you [his protégé Timothy] have known the Holy Scriptures which are able to make you wise for salvation through faith in Christ Jesus" (2 Tim 3:15). While the revelation being given through him – along with Peter, John, and others – was still being written and ultimately would become our *New* Testament, Paul is affirming to his young friend the "training in righteousness" supplied through our *Old* Testament.

Furthermore, the attempt to set aside the Old Testament as no longer needed for Christian instruction was declared *heretical* as early as 144 A.D. A Gnostic-type sect founded by Marcion rejected the Old Testament – as well as parts of the New Testament he deemed too consistent with it – as coming from a different deity than the one revealed by Jesus. His sect flourished briefly and seriously threatened the unity of the church. When someone in our own time makes comments about "the 'angry' God [of the Old Testament] who kept sending out armies to murder and pillage," that person is dangerously close to the same heretical error as Marcion.

Whether by careless reading, theological naïveté, or following the lead of someone who has taught the Old Testament poorly, one joins Marcion who says the God who is the same yesterday, today, and forever set Israelite armies or any individual to do evil. Just as Marcion thought it impossible for a loving God to visit his wrath on his human creatures, there is a robust aspect of romanticism in much modern theology that cannot abide judgment and censure as part of Christian teaching.

Yahweh's Perfect Love and Perfect Anger

I accept the Torah's self-identification of Yahweh at Exodus 34:6-7a as "the compassionate and gracious God, slow to anger, abounding in love and faithfulness, maintaining love to thousands, and forgiving wickedness, rebellion and sin." In various rehearsals of Israel's history and experiences of Yahweh, he is celebrated for his "deep compassion" and "everlasting kindness" (Isa 54:7-8). He is represented as speaking over the Chosen People to say, "I have loved you with an everlasting love; I have drawn you with unfailing kindness" (Jer 31:3).

Yet Marcion and his modern heirs cannot see the critical balance in God's character between compassionate love on the one hand and outraged holiness on the other. Each of the texts just cited brings both elements of his nature into view. In the first, Yahweh passes in front of Moses not only to proclaim abundant love and eager forgiveness but also to say: "Yet he does not leave the guilty unpunished; he punishes the children and their children for the sin of the parents to the third and fourth generation" (Ex 34:7b). Even persons who do not believe in God know it is true that certain evil actions (e.g., drug abuse, child molestation) can bring terrible consequences to both their perpetrators and their offspring for generations to come.

Isaiah knew that the prediction of Moses had come true that Israel's abandonment of the Sinai covenant had resulted in the withdrawal of divine favor (cf. Deut 28:15ff). In his anger and righteous indignation, God kept his word and "abandoned" and "hid [his] face" from them (Isa 54:7-8). And Jeremiah, the "Weeping Prophet," was living through the grief caused by the fall of Jerusalem and the destruction of its Temple in 586 B.C. – a devastation brought on by Judah's sinfulness and stubborn refusal to heed God's plea for repentance. The book named for him was nothing short of a final anguished plea for the people to repent of sins that had become so repugnant as to include both idolatry and child sacrifice (Jer 32:34-35). The poetry of Lamentations articulates his grief that the warning – which could have spared the people their terrible fate – went unheeded. Repentance could have turned away wrath.

When someone speaks of the God of the Bible as an angry deity looking for someone to punish, that person is seriously misrepresenting the facts. If one sees the armies of Israel going out to murder, rape, and plunder, that person is distorting history. The Canaanites, for example, were not driven from their land and slaughtered as a quest for living space for the offspring of Abraham but as the just punishment for a long list of sins that included not only idolatry and same-sex unions but incest, bestiality, and child sacrifice (Lev 18:24-27). Even so, this was only after they had the chance to repent over some 400 years (Gen 15:13-16). Indeed, both whole cities (Deut 20:10) and individuals such as Rahab (Josh 2) were spared upon evidence of their repentance. As a later prophet would point out, Yahweh has never taken pleasure in the death of the wicked (cf. Ezek 33:11).

Would Yahweh be the Loving God we seek to know if he did not get angry about the things that damage his offspring and deprive them of the wholesome things he wants for them? Could we consider him good if he didn't hate child molestation, poverty, and war? *He hates those behaviors because he loves the perpetrators and victims who are both persons created in his image.* Perhaps we should be careful to link our thoughts of God's anger with his grief and heartache – as the Bible does. In describing life in the days of Noah, Genesis 6:6 says the sinfulness of humankind "grieved him at his heart" (KJV) or "broke his heart" (NLT). If we are prone to think of God's wrath as his mean-spirited reaction to people he doesn't much care for anyway, that is outrageously wrong. He punishes sin because of the harm already done and the greater damage that will be done if it is not checked. That is holy love as opposed to the bloodthirsty anger of the pagan gods.

The Bible's Unified Narrative

Again, though, is this too much time and space devoted to the Old Testament, when you and I are most directly accountable to the gospel made known through Jesus in the New Testament? I think not, and here is why this is important.

First, *the God of the Old Testament is the God of the New Testament.* To use the language that opens a New Testament epistle steeped in Israel's Scripture and institutions: "In the past God spoke to our ancestors through the prophets at many times and in various ways, but in these last days he has spoken to us by his Son" (Heb 1:1-2). The Eternal Logos who became flesh both to show us God and to teach us the meaning of our humanity "is the same yesterday and today and forever" (Heb 13:8; cf. Mal 3:6). Question: Is there any evidence that the divine attitude toward same-sex behaviors changed between the time of Moses and the coming of Jesus?

Second, *the basic moral requirements of the Old and New Testaments are inescapably the same, for they are based on God's unalterable holiness.* The call of the Creator to his human creatures is "Be holy, for I am holy" – in *both* testaments (Lev 11:44-45; 1 Pet 1:15-16). Put most simply, for the same-sex behaviors so categorically denounced in the Old Testament to be permissible today would require that God's very nature be altered. Question: If God's essential nature has changed, did an imperfect deity become better or a perfect deity become less than perfect? (cf. Mal 3:6; Jas 1:17).

Third, *if the argument of some is that the prohibitions of same-sex intimacies in the Old Testament have been misunderstood and misapplied, neither Jesus, Paul, nor any other New Testament personality caught the mistake.* For that matter, the consistent interpretation of its teaching by Jews, Christians, and Muslims has been mistaken for some 3,000 years. Central to the teaching mission of Jesus was taking what "you have heard" about Torah instructions and correcting those misinterpretations and misapplications with his "but I tell you" explanations (Matt 5:21-22, 27-28, 31-32, etc.). As to the Torah itself, he stressed that its moral commands were not to be set aside (Matt 5:19). Question: Is there any evidence that Jesus challenged the universal Jewish teaching of his day that same-sex relationships were sinful?

Fourth, *the covenant shift from anticipation under Moses to fulfillment in Jesus is not the same as a Scripture shift from flawed to corrected.* We have done a disservice to ourselves in thinking of the Old and New Testaments as two stories. They are a single story in development across human history. As Motyer put it in the quotation at the top of this chapter, the Hebrew text of the Old Testament is not an "alien book" to Christians. It belongs to Christians as well as to the Jews. Paul put it this way: "For everything that was written in the past was written to teach us, so that through the endurance taught in the Scriptures and the encouragement they provide we might have hope" (Rom 15:4; cf. 1 Cor 10:11).

So let's allow the Law and the Prophets to teach us about both God's grace and judgment, about both his gifts and his warnings, about both his ideal moral standard and the pardon-renewal he offers to those who have gone wrong.

Following Up on Genesis

The most important Old Testament information about human sexual behavior has been documented already in Chapter Two. The creation narrative functions as an ethical norm by virtue of its placement at the launch of human presence in God's world and its subsequent use as a reference point for the culture to which faith calls his people. As human relationships generally (e.g., theft, violence) and marriage specifically (e.g., adultery, polygamy) are corrupted in the post-fall world, the Genesis story is offered up as the model for what human behavior *should* be. In answering a question about divorce as one of those corruptions, Jesus sensed no need to offer some new legislation or corrective. He cited the Genesis narrative as the divine norm. "Haven't you read that at the beginning the Creator 'made them male and female,' and said, 'For this reason a man will leave his father and mother to be united to his wife, and the two will become one flesh'?' (Matt 19:4-5).

On the one hand, affirming writers such as Karen Keen sees Genesis and Jesus' appeal to it as normative and mandatory for everything about marriage (e.g., no bestiality, incest, adultery, divorce, polygamy, etc.) *except* its male-female configuration.[40] And that in spite of the man-woman distinction between the partners being noted explicitly no less than five times? (Gen 1:27b; 2:22,23,24,25). The logic of such a (mis)reading is a bit mystifying. On the other hand, not one reference to male-with-male or female-with-female sexual coupling can be offered from Scripture that is not in the form of a stern denunciation. And the standard canard that such relationships in loving, committed, and monogamous form were simply non-existent and unknown in ancient times has already been proved false in the preceding chapter.

Against the claim that opposition to same-sex unions amounts to "proof-texting" based on a tiny handful of biblical texts, the reality is that these occasional negative statements are but footnotes to the Bible's thematic affirmation of male-female marriage. The storyline about marriage is that it was created and ordained by God for one man and one woman to become one flesh for one lifetime in covenantal commitment. Every negative statement about bestiality, incest, adultery, polygamy, same-sex intercourse, and the like is a boundary marker for the protection of marriage.

---

[40] Karen Keen, *Scripture, Ethics, and the Possibility of Same-Sex Relationships* (Grand Rapids: Eerdmans, 2018), 32-33.

Vines, Keen, Gushee, Scroggs, Loader, and other affirming writers have only one case to make from Scripture. It is *not* that Scripture tells the appealing and lauded story of even one same-sex pairing. It is *not* that the Bible is silent on same-sex intercourse. And it is *not* that the New Testament corrects the harsh condemnation of same-sex relationships found in the Old Testament. Their "positive case" for same-sex marriage is that Jews, Christians, and Muslims have misinterpreted the texts that only appeared to take a negative view of homoeroticism.

So we must look at those texts in turn. In this chapter, we will read and give attention to the fate of Sodom in Genesis 19 and explore the language of Leviticus about Israel's duty when a man made another male his sexual partner. If the texts are unclear or if we have inherited and institutionalized false interpretations of them, we have the right to know it.

What Was Going on in Sodom?

Vines and other revisionist writers are convinced that our English words *sodomy* and *sodomize* – the noun and verb referring to anal intercourse between males, or in some case, as synonyms for human-animal intercourse (i.e., bestiality) – perpetuate the misinterpretation of a biblical story of Sodom and Gomorrah. "Decades ago, biblical scholars on both sides of the issue dismissed the idea that homosexuality was the sin of Sodom," he writes. "Yet that belief still pervades our broader cultural consciousness."[41]

As a matter of fact, while scholars hold a variety of views about the details involved in the Sodom story, it is inaccurate to claim or imply that biblical scholarship has abandoned *en masse* the view that same-

---

[41] Vines, *God and the Gay Christian*, 60. To see that the discussion of Sodom's sin as same-sex activity is very much an *ongoing* discussion among scholars, one might wish to consult Brian Neil Peterson, "The Sin of Sodom Revisited: Reading Genesis 19 in Light of Torah," *Journal of the Evangelical Theological Society* 59, no.1 (2016): 17-31.

sex behavior is part of it. Vines insists that "the sin of Sodom had far more to do with a lack of hospitality and a bent toward violence than with any sexual designs the men had on Lot's visitors."[42] Indeed, he insists: "They were seeking to rape, and possibly kill, his guests as a show of hostility and dominance."[43]

Appealing to a later reference to Sodom in Ezekiel as "the most detailed description of the city's sins,"[44] Vines claims that the detestable things for which Sodom was destroyed focused on its arrogant lack of concern for the poor. The people of that doomed city "were arrogant, overfed and unconcerned; they did not help the poor and needy. They were haughty and did detestable things before me" (Ezek 16:49-50). Thus, he concludes, "the Bible never identifies same-sex behavior as the sin of Sodom, or even as *a* sin of Sodom."[45]

So what was really going on in Sodom and Gomorrah? Did something happen on the day the two angels in human form visited Lot's home in Sodom that stirred up mob violence? Was the intent of the people of Sodom to humiliate two strangers by raping them the reason Yahweh destroyed them? Is this really a failure of hospitality by a city already compromised by self-indulgent neglect of the poor rather than a story that focuses on sexual vice?

First, while Old Testament scholars agree that the Ancient Near East's hospitality motif is in play in this text, there is much more. Against the generous hospitality of Abraham toward three visitors in Genesis 18, two of them continued to Lot's home in Sodom and were received with appropriate hospitality by Abraham's nephew. But the text makes it quite clear that the primary violation of the city's hospitality code was sexual in nature. "Where are the men

---

[42] Ibid., 63.
[43] Ibid., 66.
[44] Ibid., 64.
[45] Ibid., 75.

who came to you tonight?" the cry was made to Lot. "Bring them out to us so that we can have sex with them" (Gen 19:4-5). That the NIV is correct to translate the Hebrew verb *yada* as "have sex" (know, KJV) is clear from the fact that the same verb is used at verse 8 when Lot makes the despicable offer of his "two daughters who have never slept with (known, KJV) a man."

Second, the destruction of Sodom and Gomorrah was not set in motion by anything that happened on the day of this visit by two messengers to Lot's family. They had been sent by Yahweh to warn Lot of a judgment that had already been decided because of the cities' persistent evils in the past. As early as Genesis 13:13, readers have been told that "the people of Sodom were wicked and were sinning greatly against the Lord." Then, at Genesis 18:20, Abraham had been told that "their sin was so grievous" that an "outcry against Sodom and Gomorrah" had come before Yahweh. The two cities had been designated for destruction well *before* the events of the visit of the two messengers. It was the announcement of their fate to Abraham that, in fact, forms the background for the founding patriarch of Israel making a plea to save Lot. Although that plea was couched in terms of an appeal that God not "sweep away the righteous with the wicked" (Gen 18:23), one has to wonder how compromised Lot and his family had become while living there. Not only did Lot offer his daughters as sexual surrogates to the mob (who, by the way, seem intent on *male* sexual contact) but those same daughters later committed rape and incest with their father (Gen 19:30-38).

Third, the New Testament makes the claim (cf. Jude 7) that it was not only the two cities of Sodom and Gomorrah but also "the surrounding towns" that were destroyed. Would Gomorrah and some nearby towns have been wrecked for the out-of-control violence of Sodom on a day two strangers showed up? Or was there some cultural pattern of vice in which the men of the region were implicated that brought down fire and brimstone? They certainly were not part of any one's day's "inhospitality" toward the two.

Interestingly, the same verse from the New Testament epistle of Jude and its parallel at 2 Peter 2:6-7 attribute the conflagration that devastated the area to "sexual immorality and perversion" or "depraved conduct of the lawless." On this point, Vines and others appeal to the quite literal "strange flesh" (Gk, *sarkos heteras*) of the KJV and NASB to claim "the phrase 'strange flesh' likely refers to the attempted rape of angels instead of humans."[46]

But were there angels visiting *all* those surrounding cities? For that matter, doesn't the text say they came not as angels but in human form as men? Finally, if they had come as angels, they would have had spirit forms rather than bodies of flesh (Heb 1:14; cf. Luke 24:37-39). As Douglas Moo and others New Testament scholars have pointed out, the noun translated "flesh" (Gk, *sarx*) would be an unlikely word to use of angels.[47] The "strange" or "other" type flesh here is more likely to indicate "flesh other than what is natural" or "flesh other than that of females" – thus a reference to same-sex intercourse among humans – rather than a type of flesh that was not really flesh at all.

Either-Or versus Both-And

But what of Vines' claim that later references to Sodom in the prophetic books of the Old Testament say nothing about either sexuality in general or any form of same-sex behavior? Here is the claim in his words. Then two responses seem appropriate.

> Of the thirteen references to Sodom in the Old Testament following Genesis 19, Ezekiel 16:49-50 offers the most detailed

---

[46] Ibid., 69.
[47] Douglas Moo, *2 Peter and Jude*, NIV Application Commentary (Grand Rapids: Zondervan, 1996), 242.

description of the city's sins. In that passage, God stated, "now this was the sin of your sister Sodom: She and her daughters were arrogant, overfed, and unconcerned; they did not help the poor and needy. They were haughty and did detestable things before me. Therefore, I did away with them as you have seen."

Sexuality goes unmentioned, both in the Ezekiel passage and in every other Old Testament reference to Sodom following Genesis 19. If Sodom's sin had indeed been same-sex behavior, it's highly unlikely that every written discussion of the city for centuries following its destruction would fail to mention that.[48]

The most obvious response to this claim is to question the unstated assumption that lies behind this take on the sin of Sodom. The "unstated assumption" is that every narrative or explanatory statement must contain the full explanation for any state of affairs. Take, for example, someone who is explaining a professional quarterback's success in the Super Bowl that resulted in his being named the game's Most Valuable Player. Let's say that Postgame Commentator Brown raves about his passing game that resulted in three touchdowns to two different receivers. He offers his view that just the right play was called at just the right time at all three critical moments and that Quarterback Jones' on-target throws were astounding. Then Commentator Green comes onscreen with equally glowing reviews of the final touchdown that sealed the victory. On fourth-and-goal at the seven, with all his receivers covered, Quarterback Jones showed his exceptional agility in sidestepping two would-be tacklers and hurtling a third to take the ball into the endzone for the game-winning score. Which analyst was right?

In that very plausible scenario about a football game – or it could have been the U.S. Open Women's Championship or the Little League World Series – I think most viewers would not have thought

---

[48] Vines, *God and the Gay Christian*, 64.

the talking heads were arguing. Brown, a former pro quarterback himself, highlighted what he knew best from his own experience. Similarly, Green spoke to what he saw from his background as an all-pro running back. We typically do not assume that anyone who speaks about a person, place, or event will focus on the same thing or highlight identical concerns. People speak out of their own backgrounds and in view of the point they are making.

Does the focus on either hospitality or sexuality in Genesis mean arrogance and the lack of social justice were non-problematic in Sodom? Does Ezekiel's concern over insensitivity and the failure of concern for others mean there was no sexual sin in the city whose history he paralleled to his own? Hardly!

In order to avoid the textual impact of Genesis – as referenced later in Jude and 2 Peter – affirming writers cite the language of Ezekiel to say the "real sin" of Sodom had nothing to do with sexual behaviors. Do you think it unlikely that a person or culture that is obsessed with sex would also be insensitive, greedy, and willing to leave the poor to fend for themselves? On the other hand, is it unthinkable to you that either an individual or group that cares little about the most marginalized of its members might also exploit them sexually? If you know anything at all about human trafficking in our own day, you know that the poor are unduly vulnerable to sexual exploitation – females and males, adults and children.

With the writer of Genesis focusing on the relationship between Abraham's family and God, the violation of their *vertical duty* of holiness before him focuses on Sodom's abandonment of sexual purity. With the prophets challenging Abraham's descendants for their self-indulgence, gluttony, and lack of brotherly compassion, they upbraided their contemporaries for following the path of trampling on others' human dignity once seen in Sodom. If Torah is keen to call out a violation of the First Command about our duty to love God in the beauty of holiness and the Prophets consistently challenge Israelite failures to the Second Command of loving neighbor, neither the Torah nor the Prophets can be faulted for a concern to name the presenting crisis of time and place.

Same-sex behavior that violates the divine mandate for sexual privilege only within marriage between one male with one female within a covenantal commitment and uncaring neglect of the elderly, impoverished, and unprotected minors were not mutually exclusive in antiquity – any more than they are in the twenty-first century. The sin of Sodom need not be taken to be *either* sexual sin *or* social injustice. History and experience in our own day tells us that *both* the preoccupation with sexual indulgence *and* a related lack of concern for the welfare of others go hand in hand.

Even so, a second response to the attempt to trump Genesis with Ezekiel – to shift the Sodom focus from same-sex activity to coldness toward those in greatest need – is to point out that Vines highlights Ezekiel 16:49 while ignoring 16:50 and omitting 16:51 in the quotation above. Here are the two verses in question: "They were haughty and did detestable things before me. Therefore I did away with them as you have seen. Samaria did not commit half the sins you did. You have done more detestable things than they, and have made your sisters seem righteous by all these things you have done."

The NIV uses the plural (i.e., "detestable things") – as do the NRSVue ("abominable things") and NASB (i.e., "detestable things") – in verse 50 to translate the Hebrew word *toevah*. In the original Hebrew text, however, the word is singular in form. Brian Peterson points out that the translators here

> . . . perhaps following the plural *anomēmata* in the LXX, confuse the translation by rendering *toevah* in the plural. However, it is in the singular, which corresponds to the singular use of *toevah* in the sex laws of Leviticus 18. In Leviticus 18, it is only the sin of homosexuality that is referred to as an "abomination" in the

singular (Lev 18:22; cf. Lev 20:13; for the plural see Lev 18:26, 27, 29, 30). What is also of importance is the fact that sexual sins are the focus when Ezekiel uses the singular *toevah* in 22:11 and 33:26. One must also remember that Ezekiel was a priest and would have been familiar with the Holiness Code of Leviticus.[49]

It is a mistake, then, to say that a literate reader would not see an allusion to same-sex behaviors in reference to Sodom outside Genesis 19. Consistent with what Paul will say centuries later in Romans, Ezekiel sees *both* social injustice *and* sexual sin as arrogance before God (i.e., idolatry) that resulted in a refusal to honor his sovereignty over all of life.

Suppose you were to see this multiple-choice question about the destruction of Sodom:

> According to the cumulative Old Testament material, the ancient city of Sodom was destroyed because of . . .
> (a) injustice
> (b) pride in its wealth
> (c) lack of concern for the poor
> (d) detestable sexual behavior
> (e) failure to show hospitality to strangers
> (f) all of the above

Against the tendency of a careless student who might choose any one of the single options (a) through (e), the correct answer would, of course, be (f). And Ezekiel's priestly use of the word *toevah* naturally takes us to the Holiness Code of Leviticus.

Leviticus: Back to Eden Again

Leviticus is hardly the favorite book of the Bible for most Christian readers. It seems at first read to be a tedious compendium

---
[49] Peterson, "The Sin of Sodom Revisited," 21.

of Hebrew rituals and detailed guidelines for observing them that are likely to induce sleep. That is an unfair caricature, however, for Leviticus is really about *relationships*. Yahweh is to be loved and revered, and neighbors are to be respected and treated ethically. Put most simply, Leviticus gives specific guidance in holiness to a people whose mindset had been shaped by slavery for generations. It is a book of *spiritual formation* for Israel. What may look to a modern reader like too great a concern for religious minutiae is actually a way of teaching the people that every facet of one's life matters to God and stands to influence his or her relationship with both God and neighbor.

Reading Leviticus from the insight of Jesus that all the Law and the Prophets are tied together by love of God and love of neighbor is a helpful approach. The first 16 chapters bring the priests and Levites (for whom the book is named in the LXX) to the fore. These opening chapters explain the right forms of worship for Israel's tabernacle (and its eventual permanent Temple) by highlighting sacrifice, priesthood, and worshippers. The remainder of the book moves outside the tabernacle to call Yahweh's worshipping people to holiness in their daily living. Leviticus is therefore at pains to say that right worship (chs. 1-16) must be combined with right living (chs. 17-27). Orthodox worship life is to exhibit its validation in upright moral life. "Be holy, for I am holy" is the keynote to the entire book (11:44-45; 19:2; 20:7,26), as Yahweh challenges Israel to live a holy life that is rooted in his own intrinsic character.

There is an important link between the creation account in Genesis and Leviticus. The tabernacle – a central feature of Leviticus – is a persistent backdrop to the laws communicated in the book. God "walked" in the garden (Gen 3:8), just as in the tabernacle (Lev 26:12); both were meeting places for Heaven and Earth, Creator and image-bearing creature. Both the original garden and the tabernacle and Temple – which were reminders of that garden – were entered from the east (Gen 3:24; Lev 27:13). Guardian cherubim were placed at the garden entrance in Genesis and embroidered onto the tabernacle entrance (Gen 3:24; Ex 26:31). Israel's "tent of meeting" was an invitation to return to Eden. Therefore, consistent with the thesis I have argued already, it is the creation narrative that defines the nature of marital partnership from Eden forward. The "abominations" of Leviticus are neither afterthoughts nor irrelevancies to ancient Israel or for us. They are aberrations from the created order.

> First, because these chapters [Gen 1-3] are a backdrop to Leviticus, it is natural to understand that the moral logic behind the Levitical prohibitions against homosexual sex is rooted in the pattern laid down in creation that helps us to understand what sex and marriage are to look like. Homosexual sex goes against this pattern, which explains why the LORD commands, "You must not have sexual relations with a male as you do with a woman" (18:22). That this pattern is being evoked would also explain why bestiality is mentioned in the very next verse (18:23); it, too, goes against the creation story, where a clear distinction is made between man and creature (Gen 1) and where the animals are brought to Adam but none is suitable to be his mate; he needs a woman (Gen 2). In both verses, the same moral rationale applies: these types of sexual relations go against God's intent for sexuality as laid out in Gen 1-2.
>
> Second, because the pattern is creational, its relevance continues today. Such an understanding is rooted in Jesus's own approach to these chapters. . . . In short, Jesus mixes the "male and female" aspect of Gen 1 right into the middle of his model for marriage. This is not what one would expect should the LORD have hoped the church would one day think of marriage only in terms of a one-flesh relationship between two people regardless of the sex of the two people in the marriage. But it is exactly what one would expect should the LORD's intent for marriage be a one-flesh relationship between two people of the opposite sex.[50]

---

[50] Jay Sklar, *Leviticus* (Grand Rapids: Zondervan Academic, 2023), 500-501; cf. 270-272.

The Holiness Code of Leviticus

Scholars typically call the second movement of the book (chs. 17-27) Israel's Holiness Code. In it are listed a variety of acts that are "detestable" (NIV) or an "abomination" (NRSVue, ESV) – ranging from dietary restrictions and touching or eating blood to incest and murder. The Hebrew word behind these translations is *toevah*. Vines argues that these behaviors are deemed to be an "abomination" by virtue of their link to pagan idolatry rather than because they are intrinsically sinful. "In the vast majority of cases, *toevah* refers to idolatrous practices of Gentiles," he claims, "which led Old Testament scholar Phyllis Bird to conclude that 'it is not an ethical term, but a term of boundary markers' with 'a basic sense of taboo.'"[51] Attaching themselves to the idea of "boundary-marking" for the Levitical prohibitions is important for affirming writers. It moves certain behaviors from the list of moral transgressions or sins to the less-than-universal class of ritual sanctions. Thus Vines concludes: "So while *abomination* is a negative word, it doesn't necessarily correspond to Christian views of sin."[52]

Why this is so critical to Vines, Boswell, Gomes, Bird, and others who argue for the moral uprightness of covenanted and caring same-sex relationships is apparent. Same-sex intercourse is specifically forbidden in two passages within the Holiness Code. "Do not have sexual relations with a man as one does with a woman;

---

[51] Vines, *God and the Gay Christian*, 85.
[52] Ibid. Revisionist interpreters such as Bird, Vines, and others rely on the work of John Boswell for this association of "detestable" acts or "abomination" with idol worship. He argued that *toevah* "does not usually signify something intrinsically evil, like rape or theft . . . but something which is ritually unclean for Jews, like eating pork or engaging in intercourse during menstruation, both of which are prohibited in these chapters [of the Holiness Code]. It is used throughout the Old Testament to designate those Jewish sins which involve ethnic contamination or idolatry and very frequently occurs as part of the stock phrase 'toevah ha-goyim,' 'the uncleanness of the Gentiles.'" John Boswell, *Christianity, Social Tolerance and Homosexuality* (Chicago: University of Chicago Press, 1980), 100. Similarly, Gomes claims that 'homosexuality is an abomination in Leviticus not because it is inherently evil, but because the Gentiles do it and is therefore ritually impure." Peter Gomes, *The Good Book* (San Francisco: HarperCollins, 1996), 154.

that is detestable" (Lev 18:22). "If a man has sexual relations with a man as one does with a woman, both of them have done what is detestable. They are to be put to death; their blood will be on their own heads" (Lev 20:13).

First, the immediate context of Leviticus 18 specifies not only having "sexual relations with a man as one does with a woman" (v.22) but adultery (v.20), child sacrifice (v.21), and bestiality (v.23) to be *toevah*. Were these "boundary-markers" peculiar to Israel? Or were they moral offenses against the holiness of God? They are clearly the latter, for "all these things were done by the people who lived in the land before you" (i.e., the Canaanites) and for which they were being driven from the land (vs.24-28). The Canaanites were not driven out for violating Israelite boundary-markers (which they would have had no idea existed!) but for their immoralities.

Second, that same-sex activity was not forbidden to Jews in order to separate them from pagans is clear from Leviticus 18:26. "The native-born *and the foreigners living among you* must not do any of these detestable (Heb, *toevah*) things." Adultery, child sacrifice, same-sex intercourse, bestiality – all these behaviors were declared evil practices for non-Jews as well as for Abraham's descendants. These behaviors are not sinful within any distinctive race, class, or sub-group or in cultic settings; they are sins at all times for all people in all contexts and in spite of any attempt at revisionist reinterpretation.

The word *toevah* is actually a broad-enough term to include "major" offenses such as idolatry or same-sex activity and relatively "minor" ones such as eating sausage or touching blood. So is there no way except our subjective impressions to determine which is a violation of God's essential holiness so that it would be forbidden under either Old or New Testament and another which might be temporary within Judaism? There are two tests that appear definitive.

Moral offenses under the Torah could incur the death penalty, whereas *ceremonial impurity* was removed by various washings, the passing of days, or a period of separation from one's family or community. Furthermore, as we will see in the next chapter, both Jesus and Paul highlighted various provisional elements of the Law of Moses that were either obsolete because of their fulfillment through Jesus or irrelevant because of the universal scope of the gospel. Yet both will specifically enjoin the permanent and universal relevance of the moral commandments that are grounded in God's essential holiness.

Finally, as to the question typically raised at this point as to why Christians don't put persons to death who violate the Bible's commandment against same-sex intercourse, the answer is uncomplicated. The Israelites in the wilderness through the time of the nation's monarchy existed as a unified church-state entity. Thus, there was no fundamental distinction between religious and civil statutes. Their violation and enforcement fell to the same juridical process. That changed when Israel became a subjected nation under another's authority. That is why, for example, the death penalty sought for Jesus by the Jewish Sanhedrin could not be carried out without authorization from the Roman official who was governing Judea. The religious charge of blasphemy had to be recast in terms of a political charge of treason.

Our modern separation of church and state does not allow the application of unique-to-faith ethical requirements to be written into civil law. Neither should Christians desire nor attempt to do so. So-called blue laws, national prohibition, mandatory prayer in public schools, criminalization of same-sex behaviors – these attempts to impose distinctive Christian views held by some or all Christian groups appear to violate basic human freedoms. While a Christian should be free to engage in public forums and to argue for their beliefs on common ground with Muslims, atheists, or even another Christian with a different point of view, he or she should not have the right to coerce others to that position.

In a first-century context where a Christian was having a sexual affair with his stepmother, Paul ordered the church to break fellowship with the man. (The woman appears not to have been a Christian, so he gave no instruction about her.) While charging the church to deal with a wayward member according to its standards, he disclaimed any right or obligation to try to enforce those values on the Greco-Roman city of Corinth. "What business is it of mine to judge those outside the church?" he asked. "Are you not to judge those inside?" (1 Cor 5:12)

In the current context of American life, church people who praise and pursue what has come to be called Christian Nationalism should pay attention to Paul's distinction.

Conclusion

The Old Testament is not the chartering document for the Christian church. It documents a time-specific, purpose-specific covenant with Abraham that has been fulfilled in Jesus of Nazareth. The document that tells of that covenant, developments involving key figures involved in its advance, and both the cultic and ethical legislation related to it remains important to Christians. Although a new covenant that is rooted in the person and work of Christ is primary to us, we need both Old and New Testaments to appreciate the work of God in history.

The narrative that begins with the creation story of Genesis sets a clear expectation for what will be blessed as appropriate sexual expression for God's human creatures. Unlike the social constructs that have variously denied certain rights to females or enslaved whole races of people, the essential nature of procreation and family structure through male-female bonding in marital commitment is affirmed and protected in Holy Scripture. There is no positive case for same-sex intercourse that can be made from the Old Testament. To the contrary, every statement in the Law and the Prophets is negative toward same-sex sexual relationships.

We move next, then, to the New Testament to explore what additional information the ministry and words of Jesus, as supplemented by the speeches and writings of his apostles and evangelists, can supply to this subject.

4

Questions for Reflection

THINK ABOUT . . .
THE CONTINUITY OF BIBLICAL REVELATION

Some of us grew up in church traditions that make far too much of the distinction between the Old and New Testaments. Looking all the way back to the Reformation, some of that may be rooted in anti-Semitism. In later generations, it was simply taken for granted that the New Testament is all we need. But the Bible is a unified story of God's work from creation to new creation. The recent idea of "unhitching" from the Old Testament is heretical.

EXPLORE . . .
2 TIMOTHY 3:14-17

What would Paul have meant by the term "Holy Scriptures" in this text? Do you hear anything in this text that could be interpreted as Paul wanting Timothy to give up the study and application of those writings? Can you name some New Testament themes that need their Old Testament roots in order to be appreciated? What does Romans 15:4 say about the value of what we call the Old Testament as a document written "to teach *us*"?

PRACTICE . . .
INFORMED INTERPRETATION OF THE BIBLE

1. Why is it necessary for the *moral instruction* God gives to be fixed and unchanging?

2. Summarize the four points made in this chapter about the Bible as a "unified narrative"?

3. Why is the Sodom story better read as a "both-and" rather than an "either-or" event?

4. What is the Holiness Code of the Old Testament? How is it linked to Genesis? Why is this so noteworthy?

5. In its treatment of sexual activities, what does the Holiness Code say about same-sex relationships? Were these "ceremonial statutes" distinctive to the Israelites?

6. What is your most important takeaway from Chapter Four?

Chapter 5 moves our study to the New Testament. The quotation setting the stage for reading it is different in tone from earlier ones. It is from a Catholic scholar who takes an affirming view of same-sex relationships. Luke Timothy Johnson admits what other affirming writers will not – that there is no ambiguity in the biblical text and one must appeal elsewhere to justify LGBTQ+ claims. Although we disagree, I can only respect his candor.

    I have little patience with efforts to make Scripture say something other than what it says, through appeals to linguistic or cultural subtleties. The exegetical situation is straightforward: we know what the text says. But what are we to do with what the text says? . . .

    I think it is important to state clearly that we do, in fact reject the straightforward commands of Scripture, and appeal instead to another authority when we declare that same-sex unions can be holy and good. And what exactly is that authority? We appeal to the weight of our own experience and the experience thousands of others have witnessed to, which tells us that to claim our own sexual orientation is in fact to accept the way in which God has created us. By doing so, we explicitly reject as well the premises of the scriptural statements condemning homosexuality – namely, that it is a vice freely chosen, a symptom of human corruption, and disobedience to God's created order.

Luke Timothy Johnson, "Scripture & experience,"
Commonweal (June 15, 2007): 15.

> *God is now acting in love and power through Jesus and by his Spirit to restore all of creation and all of human life to live again under the benevolent reign of God himself.*
>
> – Bartholomew and Goheen

5

What the New Testament Says

From Chapter Four, remember that your Bible is not two books bound together as though they were only one – Old Testament and New Testament. It is *one unfolding story* narrated in *one God-breathed Scripture* that points to *one person* who is Redeemer and Lord.

What we label the Old Testament – around 75% of the Bible's total page count – is the detailed setting within which the story makes sense. It is a multipart narrative of *anticipation* in which God's good purpose to create a world within which he could live with human beings in his own image and likeness has been thwarted by sin. Planet Earth was to be the place where God's personal splendor, creativity, abundance, companionship, and love would be experienced forever. But the lovely garden entrusted to humans has been infested with weeds.

Humankind has been banished, in fact, from the original ideal environment created for their delight and as the location for them to share with the Creator. God's response to what humans have done to spoil his original purpose was not angry destruction of the species but redemptive love. That love issued a plea and marked a path by which humans could return to the garden and live within its Creator's ideal environment as shared space. Prophets were sent to the people. Warnings against further self-seeking and rebellion were tied to visions of what yet could be. The reign of God could be established and realized on Earth as well as in Heaven. But men and women were too easily distracted to their own autonomous ends to pursue the divine agenda successfully.

Against the Old Testament promises that God would not abandon either his creation or his beloved human beings, the prediction was made about a person who would come to accomplish what the succession of prophets and seers could not. This Messiah – the "anointed one" from God – would appear and shatter the dark forces of evil with the light of his personal presence. He would prove that truth is more powerful than falsehood, moral uprightness at personal sacrifice is superior to corrupt behaviors that offer mere short-term pleasure, and that life as the Creator's gift to humankind is able to triumph over our fears of death.

The New Testament is the story of *fulfillment* by which God's original purpose will be realized at last in the New Heaven and New Earth – with all things "new" by virtue of God's never-to-be-withdrawn presence with his people. What will be experienced in that final, perfect environment is not something foreign to or amended from Eden. It will be life as it was always intended to be. All the splendor, creativity, abundance, companionship, and love of God will be shared forever with his beloved humans. Finally, the purpose of God and the dream of his prophets will be realized: "The Earth will be filled with the knowledge of the glory of the Lord as the waters cover the sea" (Hab 2:14). Again: "God's dwelling place is now among the people, and he will dwell with them. They will be his people, and God himself will be with them and be their God" (Rev 21:3).

In the meanwhile – between the launch of this final victory over evil in Jesus' personal resurrection from death and our own resurrection at his return – we pray for God's kingdom reign to come on Earth as it exists already in Heaven. We announce the opportunity to all our neighbors on Planet Earth to share in that new life by faith in Jesus. And we model, at least in our best moments, a glimpse of what that new life will be by living as determined apprentices to the Jesus-style existence that attracts people to him.

The church – not as an efficient-but-cold institution but as a warm-and-loving family – serves as an outpost of the Kingdom of God in still-hostile territory. Its family members treat one another with tender concern. They exhibit joy and peace in their demeanor. They are patient, kind, and good people. Living out their covenant faithfulness to God and one another as his children, their gentle manner simultaneously exhibits an unyielding measure of self-control that shuns the shallow indulgences so common to many of their unbelieving friends.

In a generation and culture that seems to value sexual experimentation as supreme, these Christ-followers explain their present behavior in language that sounds strange to their peers. *We believe the original placement of sexual expression in Eden remains the standard by which we are to live.*

WHAT JESUS SAID ABOUT SAME-SEX BEHAVIORS

Specific to the topic of this book, same-sex sexual experience was as foreign to Eden as jealousy, theft, or violence. It was only as first one and then another of these aberrations intruded to spoil that ideal environment – beginning with the jealousy, violence, and murder of Abel by his brother Cain – that any form of sexual intercourse beyond male-female marriage entered the flow of human behaviors.

Although it is common to hear affirming writers claim that Jesus never spoke to the issue of gay and lesbian behaviors – and therefore the church should not speak against them – I will argue that such a claim is mistaken.

If someone claims that we have no canonical record of Jesus speaking to the subject of same-sex intercourse in *explicit* language, that is correct. But we have no record in the Four Gospels of Jesus ever saying something explicit about infanticide either – or bestiality, pedophilia, child sacrifice, human trafficking, and dozens more topics that could be added to this list. Check a textbook on logic, and you'll discover that an "argument from silence" is cataloged among the logical fallacies humans sometimes embrace. Would you be persuaded, for example, that Jesus wouldn't want us to be concerned about child abuse because he never spoke against it? Or might you not say that his blessing of little children in Matthew 19:14 was an *implicit* rebuke of doing any sort of harm to them?

Second Temple Judaism was uniform and unyielding in its denunciation of same-sex acts. The alleged silence of Jesus is best accounted for by the fact that both he and his hearers presumed a shared view. When Jesus did disagree with some view commonly held within his ethnic-religious community, he tended to be at pains to point it out for correction. Moreover, that he was hardly leaving himself open to ambiguity on this subject seems clear from generic statements he made about sexual behavior. For example, in defining the nature of true defilement at Mark 7:21 and its parallel text at Matthew 15:19, Jesus names "sexual immorality." In the Greek text, the word translated as a singular term is actually plural (Gk, *porneiai*) in form. Brought into English more literally, it would be rendered "sexual immoralities" or "sex acts outside marriage." Any rabbi of the Second Temple period would have known that Israel's Holiness Code condemns a variety of sexual sins – incest, bestiality, same-sex coupling, and others. This, coupled with his endorsement of the Law's moral demands at Matthew 5:17-19, should leave no doubt in a reader's mind about Jesus' view of same-sex intercourse.

As a final observation about what Jesus taught, it cannot be insignificant that when he was asked a specific question about marriage, he responded with this: "Haven't you read that at the beginning the Creator 'made them male and female,' and said 'For this reason a man will leave his father and mother and be united to his wife, and the two will become one flesh'?" (Matt 19:4-5). The Son of Man saw an ethical imperative within the creation narrative. That "it was not this way from the beginning" (Matt 19:8) has been taken by him and his followers to apply not only to divorce but as well to additional unnamed behaviors such as polygamy, polyandry, failure to support, and the like. Can we really think the named "male and female" nature of the union is irrelevant? That though "it was not this way from the beginning," that original state of marriage implies less about *gendered* partners than about *multiple* partners?

What Paul Said about Same-Sex Behaviors

Another first-century Jew raised in the context of Second Temple teaching and attitudes toward all extra-marital behaviors was Paul. Since Paul was a diaspora Jew from the free, wealthy city of Tarsus of Cilicia – famous for its culture and intellectual sophistication – he was well-versed not only in the Torah he had studied under Gamaliel in Jerusalem but also with the far more open Greco-Roman lifestyle of his home city. In other words, this self-described "citizen of no ordinary city" (Acts 21:39) was hardly a backwater provincial who simply did not understand the challenge to his Torah values from the larger culture of the Roman Empire. When he spoke in explicit terms to the issue of same-sex pairings, not only did he not challenge Jesus on the matter of "sexual immoralities" but insisted that what he was writing to the churches had the full authority of the Lord Jesus behind it (1 Cor 5:3; 14:37; cf. 2 Cor 10:7).

Paul says more than anyone else in the New Testament about moral issues generally and sexual ethics in particular. That is understandable in view of his special mission to non-Jews in the Roman Empire. His Gentile converts in Corinth, Ephesus, and Rome didn't know the books of Moses, so he had to be very specific about teaching them a different way of life than their religions and cultures had sanctioned to them. Male citizens of the empire were generally expected to be sexually active from their teen years. Married men were not expected to be faithful to their wives. And sexual partners could be either male or female. The widespread fact of slavery across the empire made commercial sex (i.e., brothels, prostitutes) quite common. In a wealthy home where the master owned several slaves, both women and men were at his personal disposal for sexual favors – even if they had mates or children of their own.

Into this world of extreme sexual liberty for freeborn male citizens came Paul. He preached the gospel message about the identity and work of Jesus. Then, for those who embraced the new faith, he began instructing them about the lifestyle appropriate to it. As opposed now to imitating, for example, Zeus – who had sexual liaisons with both males and females – Paul taught about chastity for unmarried people and sexual exclusivity with one marriage partner. And faithfulness in marriage applied not only to wives – which Romans would have expected and required for the sake of protecting the husband's lineage and property – but to husbands as well. As one non-Christian historian puts it, what Paul taught these pagans "was a perspective on sexual relations that Roman men would barely have recognized." [53]

The essence of what he said on the subject is found in Romans 1. He also addressed it in a letter to the church in Corinth and in a pastoral letter to a younger protégé named Timothy. Because Jesus taught as a Jew among Jewish hearers, he had not deemed it necessary to address all the issues that confronted Paul among the Gentiles. In a word, Jesus simply told the children of Israel that everything taught about sexual purity in the Torah was still pertinent to them. Its basic ethical commandments, rooted as they are in the personal holiness of God, were not to be set aside but faithfully obeyed.

Paul's thesis statement for his letter to the Gentile church at Rome was that "in the gospel the righteousness of God is revealed" (1:17a). It is followed immediately by his emphatic statement that "the wrath of God is being revealed from heaven against all the godlessness and wickedness of people, who suppress the truth by their wickedness" (1:18). How can this be? God's righteousness and God's wrath are *both* being made known? Redeeming grace and divine judgment are *both* in play? And, we should notice, this is not a warning that his wrath "will be revealed" (i.e., future tense) against godlessness and wickedness. The text says his wrath "is revealed" or "is being revealed" (i.e., present tense) against sin.

The "wrath of God" Paul names here is anything but a capricious, coldhearted response from an angry deity. It is what happens unavoidably when people reject truth for lies or snub upright behaviors for wicked ones. All that is opposed to God and human wellbeing seems to be rooted in Satan's deceptions (John 8:44b), and we have been falling prey to them since Eden. God allows us to

---

[53] Tom Holland, *Dominion: How the Christian Revolution Remade the World* (New York: Basic Books, 2019), 288.

choose between truth and falsehood, but his own upright and just character then allows – or, perhaps better, requires – us to live with the consequences of those choices. Is that unjust? Unfair?

Three times in this text (vs.24, 26, 28), Paul speaks of the "exchange" we make by rejecting God for idols, holy sexuality for sexual parodies, and virtue for vice. Across time, God "gave them over" to their choices when our ancestors opted to embrace some enticing deception they had been offered. When people abandon God, however, they are by that same horrible choice left with the "wrath" of pain, chaos, shame, and dehumanization that follow. "And, moreover, the uncleanness of their relation to God submerges their lives also in uncleanness. When God has been deprived of His glory, men are also deprived of theirs."[54]

> Although they claimed to be wise, they became fools and exchanged the glory of the immortal God for images made to look like a mortal human being and birds and animals and reptiles.
>
> Therefore *God gave them over* in the sinful desires of their hearts to sexual impurity for the degrading of their bodies with one another. They exchanged the truth about God for a lie, and worshiped and served created things rather than the Creator – who is forever praised. Amen.
>
> Because of this, *God gave them over* to shameful lusts. Even their women exchanged natural sexual relations for unnatural ones. In the same way the men also abandoned natural relations with women and were inflamed with lust for one another. Men committed shameful acts with other men, and received in themselves the due penalty for their error.
>
> Furthermore, just as they did not think it worthwhile to retain the knowledge of God, so *God gave them over* to a depraved mind, so that they do what ought not to be done. They have become filled with every kind of wickedness, evil, greed and depravity. They are full of envy, murder, strife, deceit and malice. They are gossips, slanderers, God-haters, insolent, arrogant and boastful; they invent ways of doing

---

[54] Karl Barth, *The Epistle to the Romans* (London: Oxford University Press, 1933), 51.

evil; they disobey their parents; they have no understanding, no fidelity, no love, no mercy. Although they know God's righteous decree that those who do such things deserve death, they not only continue to do these very things but also approve of those who practice them (Rom 1:22-32).

In sequence, to reject the knowledge of the True God for an idol – carved or cast, material or mental – is to be given over to foolish and futile ways of thinking. (Could these new, patterned, but futile ways of thinking not be thought of as a "disposition" or an "orientation"?) Here are a few examples of the mantras that emerge from such a reorientation from God to idolatry: "I gotta be me." "Nobody can tell me what to do." "The only thing that matters in life is to be happy." "It's my life and nobody's business what I do with it." Only three weeks before writing this chapter, I was driving into Nashville on Franklin Road and read this on a church's highway marquee: "Be your authentic self." And we thought the repent-and-believe call of the gospel was that people should die to ourselves in order to be clothed with Christ! Indeed, it is not unusual these days to hear something called "gospel" that turns the Christian message on its head.

From those self-centered and Christ-rejecting mindsets, it is both natural and easy to accept that the most direct route to happiness is pleasure – most particularly, *sexual pleasure*. This is the sort of idolatry that was causing Paul such anguish of heart in Romans 1.

But Why Focus on Same-Sex Relationships?

As a Jew who had been taught the moral boundaries marked out in the Torah's Holiness Code from childhood, Paul singles out for special mention the abandonment of sanctioned male-female behaviors for same-sex relationships. Although I still meet people occasionally who think gay and lesbian companionships have come to public awareness only in modern times, Chapter Three has documented beyond question that they were well-known in the Greco-Roman world of the New Testament period. Yes, contexts varied. Yes, different attitudes toward same-sex relationships were reflected by pagan writers. But they were known and taken up as a topic of conversation in the world of Jesus, Peter, and Paul.

What readers may be inclined to miss about Romans 1 is that Paul is not simply giving commentary on the Imperial City or the bizarre things he has heard about the moral climate in Emperor Nero's household. Neither is he tracing the trajectory of a particular individual nor saying that that every consenting adult who has had a same-sex experience has done so as an act of personal defiance against God. He is offering a broad-stroke overview of human history to explain how the fundamental turn to idolatry lies at the root of all human vice.

Both Paul and I could describe some of our acquaintances who are not disciples of Jesus but who rank among the most compassionate and ethical people we know. They work to make their communities better, serve as brilliant teachers, set up programs to keep children away from drugs and sexual predators, and are faithful to their mates and children. Paul is offering a sweeping appraisal of how the larger culture of his time had come to its confused and morally shameful situation by turning from the knowledge of the God who had created them to idols.

In our own time, we love those occasional stories of heroism and sacrifice that make the news but are far more accustomed to reports of war, terrorism, human trafficking, drug addiction, gang violence, school shootings, political chicanery, and all their cousins. The proliferation of these shameful actions cannot but bring harmful effects into the cultures where they occur. The very consequences of these behaviors count as elements of God's wrath – divine judgments within history – that follow with sad but foreseeable predictably.

Although Paul names a total of twenty-two sinful behaviors that flow from turning away from God and for which human societies experience divine wrath, the most explicit and detailed of these is same-sex encounters. Why choose this as his primary case study?

> Out of the many things Paul could have highlighted in the pagan world, he has chosen same-sex erotic practices, not simply because Jews regarded homosexual practice as a classic example of pagan vice, but more particularly because it corresponds, in his view, to what humans in general have done in swapping God's truth for a lie.
>
> The underlying logic seems to be as follows. Those who worship the true God are, as Paul says elsewhere, renewed according to the divine image (Col 3:10). When this worship is exchanged for the worship of other gods, the result will be that this humanness, this image-bearing quality, is correspondingly distorted. Paul may suppose that in Genesis 1 it is male and female together that compose the image of God; or he may simply be taking it for granted that heterosexual intercourse is obviously the creator's intention for genital activity. Either way, his point is that homosexual behavior is a distortion of the creator's design and that such practices are evidence, not of the intention of any specific individual to indulge in such practice for its own sake, but of the tendency within an entire society for humanness to fracture when gods other than the true one are being worshiped. The point is: Exchange your God for an idol, and you will exchange your genuine humanness for a distorted version, which will do you no good.[55]

Having rooted his argument about the world's morally depraved state in its rejection of what is evident about God and the divine

---

[55] N.T. Wright, "The Letter to the Romans," *The New Interpreter's Bible*, Vol 10 (Nashville: Abingdon Press, 2002), 433-434. In his "Reflections" over Rom 1:18-32, Wright adds this: "Paul's comment about homosexual behavior is deeply controversial today. Attempts have been made to mitigate its force by saying (for instance) that he is only referring to a deliberate swapping from heterosexual to homosexual practice, not to what in recent years has been regarded as an innate homosexual condition, or that he was only concerned with practices related to idolatrous cults. As in some other matters, it would be wrong to press 1:26-27 for a full analysis of same-sex desires or practices; but equally it is wrong to minimalize or marginalize what Paul teaches here" (435).

nature through reflecting on his creation (Rom 1:20), Paul also links everything he says about human sexuality to the divine order of creation and to God's revealed will for human relationships.

> The reference to God as Creator would certainly evoke for Paul, as well as for his readers, immediate recollections of the creation story in Genesis 1-3, which proclaims that "God created humankind in his own image . . . male and female he created them," charging them to "be fruitful and multiply" (Gen. 1:27-28). Similarly . . . Genesis 2:18-24 describes woman and man as created for one another and concludes with a summary moral: "Therefore a man leaves his father and his mother and clings to his wife, and they become one flesh." Thus, the complementarity of male and female is given a theological grounding in God's creative activity. By way of sharp contrast, in Romans 1 Paul portrays homosexual behavior as a "sacrament" (so to speak) of the antireligion of human beings who refuse to honor God as Creator. When human beings engage in homosexual activity, they enact an outward and visible sign of an inward and spiritual reality: the rejection of the Creator's design. Thus, Paul's choice of homosexuality as an illustration of human depravity is not merely random: it serves his rhetorical purposes by providing a vivid image of humanity's primal rejection of the sovereignty of God the Creator.[56]

"NATURAL" AND "UNNATURAL" SEXUAL RELATIONS

Among the moves made at this point by revisionists who question the force of Romans 1 is an offer to redefine the distinction Paul makes between "natural" (Gk, *kata physin*) and "unnatural" (Gk, *para physin*) sexual acts. From Paul's use of the term *physin* in another of his letters, they would prefer to take his use of *kata physin* as a reference to local cultures and customs – especially with regard to expected gender roles in a highly patriarchal culture – rather than a "natural" use dictated through either biology or the will of God.

A study of Greek literature beginning with Plato reveals that the prepositional phrase *para physin* (against nature) is used by a variety

---

[56] Richard Hays, *The Moral Vision of the New Testament: A Contemporary Introduction to New Testament Ethics* (New York: HarperCollins, 1996), 386.

of persons – though seldom in their literature of ethical behaviors, for they are more likely to be discussing matters of science, physiology, and medicine – to mean "that which is against its created purpose" and not merely "outside its customary cultural setting." Thus, Aristotle allows that "nothing contrary to nature (Gk, *para physin*) is noble."[57] That Greek and Roman writers understood this language to refer to one's essential make-up rather than to something merely outside social custom has been documented carefully from the first century through the Middle Ages.[58]

Far more significant than this data concerning extra-biblical use of the terms "natural" and "unnatural" is Paul's own contextual usage. Staying in Romans, he uses the very same phrase to describe the natural growth of an olive tree and the grafting of a foreign branch into its stump in his explanation of how Gentiles have been made part of God's expanded Israel. "After all, if you were to cut out of an olive tree that is wild by nature (Gk, *kata physin*), and contrary to nature (Gk, *para physin*) were grafted into a cultivated olive tree, how much more readily will these, the natural (Gk, *kata physin*) branches, be grafted into their own olive tree!" (11:24).

Do we reasonably understand Paul to say that "wild" and "cultivated" olive trees are simply outside the ordinary? An unconventional experience? Or doesn't even the most casual reader hear the apostle contrasting what is intrinsic and native (Gk, *kata*

---

[57] Aristotle, *Politics* 7. 1325b.
[58] Cf. S. Donald Fortson III and Rolling G. Grams, *Unchanging Witness: The Consistent Christian Teaching on Homosexuality in Scripture and Tradition* (Nashville: Broadman & Holman Academic, 2016), 27-68. "Though pagan writers wrongly accused Christians of participating in perverse sexual acts, the church consistently denounced fornication, adultery, and all homosexual acts as incompatible with Christian faith. A number of the Fathers wrote commentaries on Paul's epistles and consequently dealt with the apostle's perspective on homosexuality. Early Christians condemned all practices that involved members of the same gender participating in sexual acts with one another. This included pederasty, male dominance/rape, effeminacy, lesbianism, male homosexuality, transsexuality, prostitution, temple prostitution, orgies, and homosexual 'marriages.' It was not merely a specific type of homosexual activity that was considered unacceptable, even though specific texts mentioned specific practices (such as pederasty). The church fathers condemned the immorality underlying *all* such practices" (28).

physin) to a plant with what happens when something acquired and contrary to its essential nature (Gk, *para physin*) happens to it? Wild olive trees put on branches and bear fruit according to their essential natures – unless and until something contrary to their ordered role in nature occurs. This internal-to-Romans use of the same Greek terms makes it most unlikely that he would have used vocabulary essential to these two central arguments in contrasting ways. Would that not be seriously confusing to his readers? Both in his day and in ours?

A classics scholar with no theological axe to grind on this point is unequivocal about the linguistic and historical context for Paul's language.

> For Paul, same-sex attraction symbolized the estrangement of men and women, at the very level of their inmost desires, from nature and from the creator of nature. . . . For the historian, any hermeneutic roundabout that tries to sanitize or soften Paul's words is liable to obscure the inflection point around which attitudes toward same-sex erotics would be forever altered.[59]

Earlier I mentioned a statement from Paul in another of his epistles that revisionists cite to cast doubt on the meaning of the term "unnatural" in Romans 1. That statement occurs in a letter he wrote to Corinth. "Does not the very nature (Gk, *physis*) of things teach you that if a man has long hair, it is a disgrace to him, but that if a woman has long hair, it is her glory? For long hair is given to her as a covering" (1 Cor 11:14-15). Since it has already been granted that *physis* has a wide range of meaning, it is generally deemed plausible that the meaning here could be "by custom" or "within common expectation." However, that may be too quick a concession for what Paul is saying. It is altogether possible that his comment is not a simple parallel to a mother's advice that her son should get a fresh haircut and look neat for his job interview. It well may be a

---

[59] Kyle Harper, *From Shame to Sin: The Christian Transformation of Sexual Morality in Late Antiquity* (Cambridge, MA: Harvard University Press, 2013), 94-95.

reminder that Christian men are to abstain from effeminate looks and behaviors – regardless of the latest cultural trends of Rome, Europe, or North America.

The Apostle to the Gentiles certainly knew that it was "customary" within certain cultures of his day (e.g., Parthian, German) for men to wear their hair quite long. Even within Roman culture, Paul would have been able to spot a member of the Cynic school during his Acts 17 conversation with the philosophers of Athens by their penchant for letting their hair grow long. It is equally possible, therefore, to take the term *physis* in 1 Corinthians to mean the same thing as in Romans 1 – even to hear it as an echo of his argument there. If customary practice in some cultures both observed and accepted males with long hair, there were also settings within which males with long hair signaled an effeminate disposition and willingness to engage in same-sex intercourse.

As a case in point, priests of the cult of Cybele would accept castration, dress as women, and grow long hair to appear as females. "Cybele's priests were known as the *galli*; these men wore yellow or multi-colored robes with a tiara, and 'adorned [themselves] with ornaments,' rings, and earrings; they wore white make-up and curled their long hair."[60]

One may therefore make this very plausible argument:

> Paul uses *physis* in accordance with its traditional meaning: "the way things are because they were created by God to be so." Thus, Paul's point is not that long hair is impossible for a man to grow but that an effeminate appearance for a man is unnatural. In 1 Corinthians 11:2-16, Paul is saying that men should be men and women should be women, according to nature. While hairstyles are a matter of custom, in Paul's day long hair on men suggested effeminacy in Greek and Roman culture. For a man to have long hair, then, was like cross-dressing – purposefully appearing contrary to his nature.[61]

---

[60] Anna Clark, *A History of European Sexuality* (New York: Routledge, 2008), 28.
[61] Fortson and Grams, *Unchanging Witness*, 327.

Excess or Simply Same-Sex Acts?

In Vines' *God and the Gay Christian*, his counter to the church's centuries-old reading of Romans 1 is not only the one just named in which cultural convention is claimed to be the meaning of "by nature" and "contrary to nature" but also the patriarchal context of those expectations. On his view, Paul did not understand gay orientation as a fixed element to human personality, believed that sin was always a conscious choice and could not be rooted in a fixed element of personality, and condemned same-sex activity only when it was a matter of lustful excess that violated gender expectations of the apostle's time. Let's look at this rather meandering argument in its stages of development.

First, did Paul and others from his time have any understanding of a same-sex orientation? That "the concept of same-sex orientation didn't exist in the ancient world" has been repeated so often by Vines, Gushee, Hamilton, and others that it seems established in the minds of all affirming writers and even with some who hold a traditional view. While our modern terminology about "same-sex orientation" is not in the literature of that period, the concept is there beyond reasonable doubt.

It is analogous to medieval-to-modern debates over trinitarianism. The word "Trinity" is not used in Scripture or in the earliest Christian writings about God. But the concept of three divine persons – Father, Son/Logos, Spirit – acting in concert certainly is (Matt 28:19b; 2 Cor 13:14, etc.). For that matter, Hebrew, Greek, and Latin do not have equivalent terms to our modern words "homosexual" or "homosexuality" – words that came into English from German in the late nineteenth century. We might add such words as heterosexual, gay, lesbian, transsexual, pansexual, and other terms from today's vocabulary to the list of words not found in ancient literature.

The writers of Greece, Rome, and Israel most often spoke descriptively of a "male having sex with a man as with a woman" rather than using some category term. (This is why, as stated before, I try to avoid using the word "homosexual" as a noun because it more nearly points to a preference or inclination than to a behavior in modern vocabulary. In contemporary usage, one can be a "chaste homosexual" or "chaste heterosexual." That is, her or his inclination has not been acted out so as to cross any ethical boundaries marked in Scripture.)

What we refer to as one's sexual orientation is what some writers from antiquity called their "fate" or "destiny." No less an affirming scholar than Louis Crompton examined a number of pre-Christian Greek documents and acknowledged a class of males "exclusively devoted to their own sex, approximating the modern conception of the 'homosexual.'" He concluded: "This idea of a homosexual 'orientation,' though by no means central to Greek thinking as it is to ours, was certainly understood by Plato and his contemporaries."[62] Classicist Thomas Hubbard draws the same conclusion and points out that certain sexual preferences were "considered a distinguishing characteristic of individuals. Many texts even see such preferences as inborn qualities and thus 'essential' aspects of human identity."[63]

Such references to personal sexual choices being linked to "natural disposition," fate, or other inborn traits are in the scientific, medical, and philosophical literature of the period. Since Tarsus was the third-ranked intellectual hub of its day – behind only Athens and Alexandria – is it reasonable to think such ideas would have been unknown to Paul?

Second, have we really understood Paul's point in Romans 1? Might he not have been giving approval to same-sex oriented

---

[62] Louis Crompton, *Homosexuality & Civilization* (Cambridge, MA: Harvard University Press, 2003), 57.
[63] Thomas Hubbard, *Homosexuality in Greece and Rome: A Sourcebook of Basic Documents* (Berkeley: University of California Press, 2003), 2.

relationships – while condemning only those who were experimenting with a sexuality to which they were not fit or fated?

Interestingly, even Matthew Vines grants that Paul's "description of same-sex desire in Romans 1:24-27 sounds as if he understood the desire to be innate." He adds, in fact, that "Paul seems to be describing latent desires that were being expressed, not brand-new ones."[64] So how does he argue that same-sex behavior is *not* morally wrong? How can he claim that the ancient concept of sexual orientation is somehow different from what modern psychology urges us to approve as merely a legitimate alternative lifestyle in light of its alleged insights?

Vines argues that the sin Paul denounces in Romans 1 is not same-sex intercourse *per se* but same-sex activity by persons who were opposite-sex oriented, fully capable of opposite-sex attraction and performance, but nevertheless chose to defy their customary gender role for same-sex pursuits. In other words, gay or lesbian sexual acts are wrong only when performed by persons of heterosexual orientation who are experimenting with them and attempting to "exchange" their natural opposite-sex orientation for a same-sex orientation.

The tortuous reasoning here is hard to follow. As best I can summarize it, three steps lead to a sanitizing of same-sex relationships: (a) Paul's readers would have believed that "people were thought to be capable of both opposite-sex *and* same-sex attraction" (102); (b) "Consequently, there's no reason Paul would have viewed same-sex behavior as contrary to the innate inclinations of many" (102); (c) therefore, Paul did not censure same-sex behavior *except* for those persons who "are capable of making the opposite, virtuous choice" (103). Simply put, Paul did know what we know: "Gay people cannot choose to follow opposite-

---

[64] Vines, *God and the Gay Christian*, 102. Note: Several interrelated quotations from Vines will be indicated within this chapter by putting page numbers in parentheses immediately after the quoted material.

sex attractions, because they have no opposite-sex attractions to follow – nor can they manufacture them" (103).

Vines' attempt at structuring an affirming argument fails badly here. For one thing, it is not the decision to "exchange" their true orientation for another that is the root of Paul's judgment against same-sex coupling. The "exchange" is the result of their prior refusal to honor God which, in turn, caused their thinking to become "futile" and their hearts to be "darkened" (Rom 1:22). It was this prior rejection of God that garbled their spiritual sensitivities which had unleashed God's wrath in the present time (i.e., "is being revealed," 1:18) which resulted in their being given over to sinful desires and shameful lusts. The exchange of natural for unnatural sexual behavior was *the result of their prior sin of turning from God.* It was not the root sin of a few that could have negative consequences for them.

For another, since we know that alternative sexual lifestyles – including long-term, committed, authentically caring, and mutually supportive same-sex partnerships – have been around from antiquity into our own time, biblical sanctions against any and all sexual intercourse outside the Edenic norm explored earlier have been always and only against deviant (i.e., unnatural) *acts* – without regard for their actual or alleged motivations.

In Holy Scripture, the issue is the act – and vice versa. Polygamy is wrong, even if a surplus of female presence in a war-torn land has left countless women without a male protector. Incest is wrong, even if the father's wife and natural sexual companion is so seriously ill or badly injured that she cannot have sex with him. Prostitution is sinful, even if there is no work to be found by a woman who needs income to survive. And same-sex intercourse is forbidden, even if one's greater comfort with and inclination toward is with her or his own gender.

Third, was the real sin Paul castigated "sexual excess" rather than same-sex intercourse *per se*? Vines makes this rather fantastic claim about Romans 1. "Paul wasn't condemning the expression of a same-sex orientation as opposed to the expression of an opposite-sex orientation," he informs us. "He was condemning *excess* as opposed to *moderation*" (105). As to what "excess" would have been in Paul's day, he sees it as the sort of thing that happened "because they've grown tired of heterosexuality and are seeking a new outlet for their insatiable lusts" (106-107).

It is certainly correct to say that "insatiable lusts" appear to drive much of the sexual culture and behavior of modern times. It was surely the same in ancient times as well. And those lusts and the fruits they bear are wicked. But it stands Paul on his head – along with the Torah and its creation-narrative of marriage and sexuality he had been taught and was mirroring in Romans 1 (see v.20 in particular!) – to make this claim: "Same-sex behavior condemned as excess doesn't translate to homosexuality condemned as orientation – or as a loving expression of that orientation" (106).

The claim is not credible in view of the fact already documented in Chapter Three that there are numerous same-sex relationships that were exclusive, committed, and caring that are known to us. They were not formed by bored and experimenting souls who were burned out with bedding the opposite sex. Obvious examples would be Athenian and Spartan pederastic pairs who continued their exclusive bonds through their adult years, the paired lovers of the Sacred Band, Emperor Galba, or Hadrian and Antinous.

"Men Who Have Sex with Men"

Against the backdrop of Greco-Roman sexual permissiveness, Paul wrote a letter to the church at Corinth with some very specific guidelines about purity. He both rebuked the church for its lenient attitude toward one of its men who was involved in a sexual relationship with his stepmother (1 Cor 5:1-11) and for some who appear to have been seeking out prostitutes for themselves (1 Cor 6:12-20).

A third sexual aberration – whether actual or potential among believers – is also named in the letter's sixth chapter. Beginning with the very broad category term "wrongdoers," the apostle names some specific acts that such persons commit.

> Or do you not know that wrongdoers will not inherit the kingdom of God? Do not be deceived: Neither the sexually immoral nor idolaters nor adulterers nor men who have sex with men nor thieves nor the greedy nor drunkards nor slanderers nor swindlers will inherit the kingdom of God (1 Cor 6:9-10).

The reference to "men who have sex with men" translates two words from the original text. One of them (*malakoi*) is known to us from Greek literature outside the Bible (e.g., Philo, Diogenes Laertius, Pseudo-Lucian) to mean "something soft" or a "soft person" – apparently referring to the passive male partner who takes the feminine (receptive) role in the sexual encounter. English translations of those passages in non-biblical works sometimes use the word "effeminate" or "depraved." The other term is not found in any Greek literature known to us before Paul's use of it here. He apparently coined the word *arsenokoitai* by fitting together two words found both in Leviticus 18:22 and 20:13 in the Septuagint – *arsenos* (male) and *koitēn* (bed). The result is an invented word that means "man-bedder" or "a man who lies with a man." Whether invented or chosen by Paul, the word echoes the wide-ranging condemnation of same-sex couplings found in the Holiness Code of Leviticus.

It is this background for the two words that produced a footnote to the NIV's translation of 1 Corinthians 6:19: "The words *men who have sex with men* translate two Greek words that refer to the passive and active participants in homosexual acts." Thus Paul cannot be said to be using a narrow term that specifies pederasty, male prostitution, master-slave sexual abuse, or anal rape. There were words in the Greek vocabulary of his day already for all those. Instead, he employed or perhaps even fashioned an expansive word that included all those offenses and then went beyond them to make sure it covered even the sexual exchanges among consenting adults that were loving, committed, and enduring in nature.

Vines seeks to avoid this linguistic information and its implications by repeating his already-refuted assertion that "While *malakoi* and *arsenokoitai* could encompass forms of same-sex behavior, the behavior they might describe bears little resemblance to the modern relationships of lesbian, gay, bisexual, and transgender Christians" (130). To continue repeating the claim that ancient writers knew nothing of committed, long-term, monogamous, and loving same-sex relationships disregards what history, archaeology, art, and literature from the period show beyond doubt. Repeating a false claim does nothing to establish it as truth. Instead, it shows the determination to cling to a conclusion in spite of the evidence.

Conclusion

It would be a mistake to end this chapter on what the New Testament says about same-sex behaviors without following the passage from 1 Corinthians through to its conclusion. In Christian teaching, any word of judgment or condemnation that must be spoken always implies the possibility of grace and redemption. After all, the entirety of Scripture stresses that God is always about the work of saving, not destroying. So, in the earlier part of the Bible as a single story, the Old Testament has Yahweh saying to Israel, "I take no pleasure in the death of the wicked, but rather that they turn from their ways and live" (Ezek 33:11b). The heart of God for his erring people is the same in the New Testament documents: "The Lord is patient with you, not wanting anyone to perish, but everyone to come to repentance" (2 Pet 3:9b).

After warning believers in Corinth about certain behaviors – including but not limited to men having sex with other men – that bring about exclusion from the Kingdom of God, one hears Paul's voice rise in celebratory joy to add: "And that is what some of you were. But you were washed, you were sanctified, you were justified in the name of the Lord Jesus Christ and by the Spirit of our God" (1 Cor 6:11).

God's redeeming and emancipating grace is more effectual than any bondage sin has established in a person's life. What was true in Corinth long ago is still true where you are today. God has sought to protect the marriage-and-family configuration he created by barricading it against any other sexual partnership. The divine prohibitions are not designed to limit or deny us but to fashion pure hearts, dignified behavior, and healthy relationships.

5

Questions for Reflection

THINK ABOUT . . .
THE ORIGINAL RECIPIENTS OF
NEW TESTAMENT ETHICAL INSTRUCTION

The Gospels tell us of the moral instructions of Jesus principally in terms of his clarification of the Decalogue and other Jewish literature. His ministry – and that of the early church for perhaps ten years – was "to the Jew first and then to the Gentiles." When Peter and Paul began expanding the church's outreach to Gentiles, they could no longer presume knowledge of the Torah. Thus the more explicit teaching about sexual behavior is in their letters.

EXPLORE . . .
1 PETER 2:18-25

The question section for Chapter One looked at 1 Peter 2:11-17 – an apostle's challenge to people whose past had been in paganism to live now to the high standard of Judeo-Christian ethics. Beginning at 2:18 (and going through 4:19), he shifts to the matter of suffering at the hands of masters, husbands, and others still living as pagans. Try to imagine the many situations (including sexual ones) that would have brought abuse to these new converts.

Practice . . .
Informed Interpretation of the Bible

1. How does this chapter explain Jesus' lack of explicit teaching on topics such as incest and same-sex acts?

2. Why would Paul's letters to non-Jewish churches contain explicit instruction on sexual behaviors?

3. Give your understanding of why Paul focuses on same-sex activity in Romans 1.

4. What does Paul say about "natural" and "unnatural" sex acts? Does his point appear difficult or obscure?

5. Paul's positive note at 1 Corinthians 6:11 is vitally important. While being honest and forthright about what the Bible says about sexual sin, we must never fail to balance it with the message of redemption.

6. What is your most important takeaway from Chapter Five?

Chapter 6 explores some of the rapid and radical changes in ethical theory and practice that have come about in Western civilization. In particular, views of human sexuality have changed at lightning speed. The following quotation from a "secular source" zeroes in on one of those troubling ethical earthquakes.

Once a rare diagnosis, [gender dysphoria] has exploded over the past decade. In England and Wales the number of teenagers seeking treatment at the Gender Identity Development Service (GIDS), the main clinic treating dysphoria, has risen 17-fold since 2011-12. An analysis by Reuters, a news agency, based on data from Komodo, a health-technology firm, estimated that more than 42,000 American children and teenagers were diagnosed in 2021 – three times the count in 2017. Other rich countries, from Australia to Sweden, have also experienced rapid increases. . . .

Almost all America's medical authorities support gender-affirming care. But those in Britain, Finland, France, Norway and Sweden, while supporting talking therapy as a first step, have misgivings about the pharmacological and surgical elements of the treatment. A Finnish review, published in 2020, concluded that gender reassignment in children is "experimental" and that treatment should seldom proceed beyond talking therapy. Swedish authorities found that the risks of physical interventions "currently outweigh the possible benefits" and should only be offered in "exceptional cases." In Britain a review led by Hilary Cass, a pediatrician, found that gender-affirming care had developed without "some of the normal quality controls that are typically applied when new or innovative treatments are introduced." In 2022 France's National Academy of Medicine advised doctors to proceed with drugs and surgery only with "great medical caution" and "the greatest reserve."

"The evidence to support gender transitions is worryingly weak," *The Economist* (April 8, 2023): 15-17.

We shall soon be in a world in which a man may be shouted down for saying that two and two make four, in which furious party cries will be raised against anybody who says that cows have horns, in which people will persecute the heresy of calling a triangle a three-sided figure, and hang a man for maddening a mob with the news that grass is green.

– G.K. Chesterton

6

Why Perspectives Have Changed

There has been a seismic shift in public attitude toward gays, lesbians, and same-sex marriage in the past three decades. While people generally change their minds rather slowly to embrace major societal shifts (e.g., women's rights or racial desegregation in the United States), social scientists agree that the normalizing of same-sex relationships has taken place with a swiftness unlike any other in modern times.

In polling by the Pew Research Center in 2004, a majority of the American public opposed same-sex marriage by 60%, while only 31% approved it. In no more than 15 years, the same polling group found those percentages had reversed – with 61% expressing support for same-sex marriage and 31% opposing it.[65] Commenting on such a remarkable change, a political science professor at the

---

[65] "Attitudes on Same-Sex Marriage," *Pew Research Center*, May 14, 2019, https://www.pewresearch.org/religion/fact-sheet/changing-attitudes-on-gay-marriage.

University of Kansas, Don Haider-Markel, said, "You can't find another issue where attitudes have shifted so rapidly."[66]

It is not only the public attitude as measured by "secular" researchers that has changed over that short length of time. The posture adopted by denominations – both "mainline" and "evangelical" – has also changed. "Just five years ago it would have been okay to say homosexuality is a sin and an abomination," said Brandon Robertson. "Today you would be hard-pressed to find any major evangelical leader who would say that publicly."[67]

It is generally known that the United Methodist Church has undergone a significant split between its conservative members who wanted to retain their commitment to the church's historic position on sexuality as their denomination's leadership moved to an affirming view. Its General Conference supported traditional marriage in 2004 by endorsing "laws in civil society that define marriage as the union of one man and one woman" with 70% of the vote. Yet there were Methodist pastors performing same-sex ceremonies in defiance of their church's *Book of Discipline* and retaining their pastorates. Has that denomination's liberal drift that created the Global Methodist Church in 2022 given legitimacy to the criticism that the only thing conservatives care about is sexual issues? Some make that very claim. After all, United Methodist bishops and ordained clergy had been voicing skepticism about the virgin birth and bodily resurrection of Christ before taking up the banner of same-sex marriage.

This chapter proposes to identify some of the more significant factors that have contributed to this changed perspective on LGBTQ+ behaviors – including, but not limited to, same-sex marriage.

---

[66] Samantha Schmidt, "Americans' views flipped on gay rights. How did minds change so quickly?" *Washington Post*, June 7, 2019, https://www.washingtonpost.com/local/social-issues/americans-views-flipped-on-gay-rights-how-did-minds-change-so-quickly/2019/06/07/ae256016-8720-11e9-98c1-e945ae5db8fb_story.html.
[67] Ibid.

Our Cultural Sexual Ethic: Moralistic Therapeutic Deism

America is now a post-Christian culture where much of what survives as religion is a remix made up of a little Bible, a larger dash of pop psychology, and defining quantities of self-validating egoism. Thus some of the strongest of "faith statements" from people I have met lately take some form resembling this: "I could never believe in a God who *x*!" – where *x* is in disagreement with the speaker's view or makes an unwanted and unwelcomed demand on that person's life choices.

Two sociologists have given us what has become a widely used name for this vague and undemanding disposition. Christian Smith and Melinda Lundquist Denton have dubbed it "Moralistic Therapeutic Deism." Their research[68] focused on the core religious beliefs of American teenagers at the turn of the century, but their findings have come to be regarded by many as the general state of cultural beliefs in our country. In brief summary:

- A god exists who created and ordered the world and watches over human life.
- People should be good, nice, and fair (i.e., moral) in dealing with each other.
- The central goal of life is to be happy and to feel good about oneself.
- There are no absolute moral truths for a human life.
- God does not need to be particularly involved in one's life, except when needed to resolve a problem.
- Good people go to heaven when they die.

To some of the central questions about faith, a common answer was a shrug of the shoulders and a verbal, "Whatever." All

---

[68] Christian Smith and Melinda Lundquist Denton, *Soul Searching: The Religious and Spiritual Lives of American Teenagers* (New York: Oxford University Press, 2005).

this leads me to claim that the most critical question for the sort of study this book has offered is epistemological. If you don't know the word, *epistemology* is the study of knowledge and its sources. Put most simply for our purposes: *What do you regard as "truth" about any ethical issue? Where do you look? What would count as an authoritative source of information?*

Whether male or female, gay or straight, believer or non-believer – we simply go round and round again in disagreement about what will count as reliable information on the subject under discussion. If anyone hasn't picked up on it from the first five chapters of this book, my conviction is that the 66 books of canonical Judeo-Christian Scripture constitute the narrative account of who we are and set the norms for the persons we are called to be.

The ethical standards found in the Bible are much more than some casual "whatever" to Christians. They are obligatory standards that are grounded in God's own character (i.e., his holiness) and given to us out of concern for us (i.e., his love). Within the larger civil and criminal laws that govern the society in which Christians live, we accept the obligation to obey those laws within our understanding of Scripture. Christians in the United States are to pay our taxes and drive on the right side of the highway. These laws reflect a *shared societal ethic* to which we are accountable.

In addition, Christians acknowledge a *distinctive Christian ethic* that calls us to certain behaviors we should not bind on others by means of our shared societal ethic. For example, confessing Christ as Savior and giving money to our faith communities or forbidding marital infidelity and same-sex marriage should not be forced on unbelievers – even if a majority of Christians could vote them into the statute books. This is a distinction some Christians seem not to have grasped at times – and whose subsequent actions have offended and frightened non-Christians. Christians must exhibit love for our unbelieving neighbors without trying to force our distinctive beliefs on them. The Christian faith is to be shared and advanced by *persuasion*, not coercion.

Go back, then, to the opening paragraph of this chapter and its comment about the "normalizing" of LGBTQ+ behaviors generally and same-sex marriage in particular. If non-Christians (appropriately!) have taken offense to and faced coercion by blue laws, compulsory prayer in public schools, and diversion of public funds to specifically religious purposes, the tables have been turned of late. A blatant media bias has depicted Christians in the most unfavorable light for our views on issues such as marital infidelity, abortion on demand, and same-sex marriage. From media journalists to popular sitcoms to celebrity entertainers and athletes, the sort of name-calling that would not be allowed on an elementary school playground is routine. To be called bigots and represented as self-righteous buffoons is standard fare. While Christians sometimes have been bigoted and self-righteous, the emotive treatment of some distinctive tenet with a mere wave of the hand seems – well, bigoted and self-righteous.

"So why can't you Christians just love everybody and leave your ridiculous beliefs out of it?" someone repeats. Again, the caricature (i.e., ridiculous beliefs) seems to reflect some of the intolerance we Christians have been guilty of at times – and which embarrasses those of us who want to have rational conversations about topics we see as important. For one, I want to defend the personal dignity and legal rights of my neighbors who are atheists, Buddhists, or Muslims. I have done the same in the past – and will continue doing so – for my workplace friends who are cohabiting without being married or living in my neighborhood as a same-sex couple. Might I weigh in on public discussion of public school policy if transgendered teens are being allowed to compete with my daughter in athletics? Almost surely. Might I lobby to have transgendered students expelled from her school? No. Would I run for office or support a candidate whose purpose is to write my distinctively Christian views about same-sex marriage into law? No.

This book is an appeal for Christians – and persons sympathetic to Christian values – to understand why it is an abandonment of distinctive Christian ethics to move away from the views of chastity outside of and fidelity within male-female marriage and is to reject the authority of the Word of God. That move puts the spiritual welfare of souls in jeopardy.

Three Distorted Ethical Principles

It is my view that what Smith and Denton have identified and characterized arises from three reasonable points of departure that, when distorted and taken to their extremes, have made Moralistic Therapeutic Deism inevitable. Those same extremes are contradictory to the Christian faith and its call to follow Jesus. Together, they have spawned five cultural factors that have combined to alter our generation's perspective on same-sex relationships and acts.

Autonomy. Our English word "autonomy" is derived from two Greek terms – *auto*, meaning self, and *nomos*, referring to law. In ethics, it refers to one's right to make ethical decisions without coercion. Usually stated as a negative, autonomy means one must not have his or her free will violated without sufficient justification. Parents may decide for a small child to have her tonsils or appendix removed because a four-year-old girl does not have the knowledge or life experience to understand why an unpleasant thing must be done. But a 37-year-old woman may refuse all treatment for her life-threatening cancer because of her ability to understand the consequences of doing so. So far, so good. Autonomy means that a responsible adult is free to make his or her own decisions without coercion.

There is, however, a type of *radical autonomy* that is neither good nor tolerable. All of us live within spheres of responsibility that require us to self-limit our privacy and rights. Citizens, family members, business partners, university students – all of us enter into social contracts, whether stated or implied, that entail voluntary limits on what we will do. That "I just wanted to do it" is not a sufficient legal or ethical defense for yelling fire in a crowded room or "I thought it would be fun" for torturing animals. This take on personal freedom reminds people who know the Bible of the chaotic time in Israelite history when "everyone did as they saw fit" (Judg 17:6; 21:25).

With regard to sexual relationships, radical autonomy says, "This is my life and my body, so I have the right to do as I please." How many times have we heard that in movies and in real life? But one who understands the commitment made in becoming a Christian has a profoundly different view of life generally and the human body in particular. As a disciple of Jesus, radical autonomy has been abandoned for the sake of faithful obedience.

"You are not your own; you were bought at a price," wrote Paul to some sexual libertines at Corinth. "Therefore honor God with your bodies" (1 Cor 6:19b-20). No matter my sexual orientation or your strong attraction to certain behaviors, the fact that a Christian belongs to God demands accepting his norms for our actions. What a profoundly opposite point of departure for sexual ethics that is from our generation's mantra about absolute personal freedoms.

Mutual consent. Closely related to and growing out of the autonomy principle is the issue of consent. Even in a non-Christian culture that embraces radical autonomy for adults, there is general agreement that one cannot force his or her desire on another equally autonomous person. In sexual encounters, the violation of another's will to participate in intercourse is rape – whether the exchange is between married or unmarried, straight or gay persons. The importance of consent in our culture has been stated this way in the popular press:

> In our post-sexual-revolution culture, there seems to be wide agreement among young adults that sex is good and the more of it we have, the better. That assumption includes the idea that we don't need to be tied to a relationship or marriage; that our proclivities are personal and that they are not to be judged by others — not even by participants. In this landscape, there is only one rule: Get consent from your partner beforehand.[69]

Again, from a Christian perspective on moral responsibility, one would agree that nonconsensual sex is wrong (i.e., rape), but that hardly justifies anything that one's partner consents to share (e.g., premarital sex, adultery, incest). Consent merely allows what is otherwise morally permissible but cannot make virtuous a behavior that is forbidden in and of itself. This gets us back to the sometimes-muddy waters of a Christian defending someone's civil and legal right to engage in certain behaviors that are forbidden to Christians.

By analogy, it is legal to tell a lie about someone – politicians are notorious for doing it with impunity – but immoral nonetheless. With regard to sex, it is legal for "consenting adults" to pursue any number of sexual exchanges that the Bible says are morally wrong and forbidden. As this book has documented, all same-sex intercourse is forbidden in all settings. It is not a partner's consent that makes sexual contact acceptable. The issue for Christians is approval within God's will. One's civil or legal right to do something is one thing, while a Christian's moral right to do that same thing is often quite another.

---

[69] Christine Emba, "Consent is not enough. We need a new sexual ethic," *Washington Post*, March 17, 2022, https://www.washingtonpost.com/opinions/2022/03/17/sex-ethics-rethinking-consent-culture.

Self-interest / pleasure. Then there is the issue of personal satisfaction in life. It is not an evil thing to take care of one's health, play golf or tennis, cheer for your favorite football team, or otherwise have a good time. The pleasure humans derive from a good meal, hanging out with friends, doing meaningful work, or cheering for a favorite team is delightful icing on the cake of life. Like children who want their total diet to consist of ice cream and cake icing, however, people who make having fun their goal for living become unhealthy and may die to all sense of moral accountability. It happens all too often in human experience when earning good money morphs into greed or legitimate authority turns into bullying and abusive behaviors.

What can happen with money and power likely occurs even more frequently with sex. Not everyone amasses enough of a fortune to live the "party life" – even if desired and pursued. Neither do many people achieve a level of authority in business or public life to "throw their weight around" by threatening and mistreating their subordinates – although, again, they may do so in their small circle of family and friends, church contacts or gang members. Sex, however, stands to be a pleasure available to people at every level of economic or social standing.

Sex is pleasurable by God's design, but pleasure is not the purpose for which God created us as sexual beings or its goal in Christian experience. The Genesis account of creation has God linking male-female sexual expression most directly to human procreation – "be fruitful and increase in number" (Gen 1:28). The Creator designed the experience to generate pleasure and intense personal bonding between the partners. The one-flesh intimacy between one man and one woman over time becomes a significant aspect of "making love" between the two. It is the highest experience of physical intimacy two people can have in becoming "one flesh" within the will of God.

As with money and power, when sex is separated from the purpose for which it was intended, it is corrupted. When sex is one's selfish pursuit of pleasure or even a display of true romantic love that is willing to set aside biblical teaching, it becomes a pale imitation of God's intention.

It is the Genesis narrative that reveals God's ideal will and establishes the norm for human sexual expression. Living in the fallen world of Genesis 3 and beyond, his people in the days of ancient Israel and the modern church are called to reject all the imitations of the ideal for the sake of honoring what is holy. Just as Jesus appealed to the creation story as normative on the issue of divorce in Matthew 19, we must follow that same approach in the matter of male and female as the exclusive sexual pattern for one-flesh union in a covenanted marriage. Not only did Jesus *not* abolish the theology of creation to authorize what had been forbidden in the Torah, but he also affirmed it emphatically – as did Paul and the early church.

Autonomy, consent, and self-interest are reasonable – and biblically defensible – points of departure for framing one's moral life. Taken to the extremes just named and illustrated, though, they have produced at least five major cultural shifts in the past half century that are responsible for the surprisingly swift change of attitudes with respect to sexual morality.

Cultural Shift #1:
The Postmodern Mindset

Since the late twentieth century, Western civilization has been a *Postmodern* culture. One of the several hallmarks of that culture is the elevation of feelings over facts. Facts-out-there have given way to feelings-in-me/us. A well-told story is worth more than an encyclopedia filled with mere facts. Authority resides in each person or chosen subset of persons. In a Postmodern world, nobody has the right to tell anyone else what is true, right, or obligatory.

In 2016, Oxford Dictionaries declared "post-truth" their international word of the year. It is an adjective that means "relating to circumstances in which objective facts are less influential in shaping public opinion than emotional appeals." When the word was introduced, Casper Grathwohl, Vice President and Publisher of Reference at Oxford University Press gave his opinion that the word could become "one of the defining words of our time." As reported by the BBC, Mr. Grathwohl pointed to the rise of social media as a news source and the widespread distrust of information offered by governments, scientific groups, and universities. The combination of these factors has allowed terms such as "post-truth politics" to enter our public discourse.[70]

I fear the famous dictionary publishers are correct. Our Postmodern culture is steeped in – no, perhaps better – drowning in *relativism*. How often do we hear language these days such as "That may be true for you, but that doesn't mean it is true for anybody else" or simply "You and I clearly have different truths." *Really?* What at first may sound broad-minded and tolerant could be the loss of an opportunity for a really helpful conversation.

If "your truth" signals that you are reporting your feelings about a person or situation, so be it. In that case, more precise language would be something like "My emotional take on that is . . ." or "My gut reaction to his claim is . . ." But that is not what the word truth means – at least, not in Christian vocabulary or in thoughtful conversation among serious adults. When a flat-earther or Holocaust denier speaks "his truth" on those subjects, he is simply telling you what he chooses to think about a subject

---

[70] "'Post-truth' declared word of the year by Oxford Dictionaries," *BBC News*, November 16, 2016, https://www.bbc.com/news/uk-37995600.

and announcing his rejection of what is generally regarded as established fact or the actual set of circumstances.

While we cannot deny each other the right to our personal opinions, an opinion is not a truth. An opinion or personal belief is elevated to the status of "truth" when it has been justified by a substantial weight of evidence. Even then, especially in science, a given truth of quantum mechanics may need refinement and tweaking. With regard to events, however, they either did or did not happen. With regard to a word or statement in context, one is either correct or incorrect.

Unless a person chooses to live in a bubble where everyone yields to the opinion of a single voice or chooses to define words in ways contrary to their standard usage, "my truth" and "your truth" are simply shorthand ways for avoiding healthy discussion. "My truth" becomes what one pundit defined as a "pretentious substitute for 'non-negotiable personal opinion.'"[71] If we were to use the language of Plato and Aristotle or Jesus and Paul, we might spell the word Truth with a capital letter, say it is something to seek outside oneself, and that our moral duty is to align our sentiments and attitude with it. In the Postmodern era, where "post-truth" describes a mindset, things have changed. The claim of absolute truth about anything is regarded as an intimidation tactic in one's bid for power. Thus the truth that matters is inside oneself and cannot be the subject of another's challenge. To disagree with someone's "personal truth" is not only in poor taste but may well be considered an act of hatred.

For someone who has exchanged Truth for "my truth," the goal of life could never be "Seek first God's kingdom and his righteousness" (Matt 6:33) but "Be true to yourself by following your heart in all things." That mantra might remind you of an ancient proverb you

---

[71] "My Truth," *Urban Dictionary*, https://www.urbandictionary.com/define.php?term=My%20Truth.

have likely heard before. And, wouldn't you know it, that proverb comes right out of the Bible: "There is a way that appears to be right, but in the end it leads to death" (Prov 14:12).

It is this Postmodern mindset that has brought us to the point that fixed moral truths about sex between teenagers, marital infidelity, polyamory, gay and lesbian relationships, and same-sex marriage cannot be presented – without the presenter being branded a judgmental bigot. Yet how can one be considered a Christian without embracing a source of truth greater than his or her own feelings? Is the Bible a revelation of the mind and will of God? Or is it merely a collection of the subjective impressions of ancient writers that may be set aside at will by the subjective sense of present-day readers?

CULTURAL SHIFT #2:
A SCENARIO FOR NORMALIZATION

The shift to a Postmodern, post-truth, and post-Christian mindset is the broad cultural movement within which a focused strategic plan was outlined for normalizing same-sex relationships in mainstream American culture. Activists for what they termed "gay rights" – piggybacking the term "civil rights" and aligning themselves with the legitimate challenge to racial segregation of the time – articulated a specific way to persuade people simultaneously to see same-sex coupling as just an "alternative lifestyle" and traditional Christian morality as "out of step with the times" and advanced only by "homohating churches." A book review in the *Los Angeles Times* at the time of its release called it a "provocative call to arms on gay rights" and quoted its authors' intent to offer "a practical agenda for bringing to a close, at long last, the seemingly permanent crisis of American homosexuality."

Instead, they have devised a program of gay advocacy based on media-wise techniques of image manipulation: "A continuous flood of gay-related advertising" that will depict gays "in the least offensive fashion possible" while making "homohating beliefs and actions look so nasty that average Americans will want to dissociate themselves from them." This is pure propaganda, of course, but it is propaganda on the highest levels of insight and calculation.

"We have in mind a strategy as calculated and powerful as that which gays are accused of pursuing by their enemies – or, if you prefer, a plan as manipulative as that which our enemies themselves employ," Kirk and Madsen declare. "It's time to learn from Madison Avenue, to roll out the big guns."[72]

Expanded from a 1987 magazine article titled "The Overhauling of Straight America," two men teamed up to publish the book in 1989 that laid out a scenario by which same-sex behavior could move from closeted shame to public approval. Although gay activists deny any elements of a "gay agenda" in the book, it certainly laid out – perhaps simply as a hopeful scenario – how a whole country's mindset about gay and lesbian behaviors could be transformed. In its review of the book, *Publisher's Weekly* dubbed it "a punchy call to arms, Madison Avenue style."[73]

In the magazine piece, what the writers themselves labeled a "blueprint" for a desired outcome of a changed social perspective toward lesbian and gay persons is made clear. "We have sketched out here a blueprint for transforming the social values of straight America," they wrote. "At the core of our program is a media campaign to change the way the average citizens view homosexuality."[74] As to what the Bible says about same-sex behaviors,

---

[72] Jonathan Kirsch, "Book Review: A Provocative Call to Arms for Gay Rights," *Los Angeles Times*, Oct 4, 1989, accessed at https://www.latimes.com/archives/la-xpm-1989-10-04-vw-693-story.html.

[73] Publishers Weekly Book Review, Aug 29, 1990, https://www.publishersweekly.com/9780452264984.

[74] Marshall Kirk and Erastes Pill (pen name used by Hunter Madsen), "The Overhauling of Straight America," *Guide Magazine*, Nov 1987, accessed at https://library.gayhomeland.org/0018/EN/EN_Overhauling_Straight.htm.

the same article promoted "raising serious theological objections to conservative biblical teachings." Gay and lesbian persons were urged to "undermine the moral authority of homohating churches . . . by portraying such institutions as antiquated backwaters, badly out of step with the times and with the latest findings of psychology." Two years later, the article had grown into a full-length book published by Doubleday.

The activist authors brought together the two disciplines most relevant to their announced goal. Hunter Madsen was a bright, Harvard-educated student of persuasion, psychology, and propaganda. He met Marshall Kirk during his Harvard years, where Kirk was studying psychology. The two became a formidable pair in their *After the Ball: How America Will Conquer Its Fear of Gays in the '90s*.[75] Using the term "propaganda" of their project, the book proposed a Waging Peace Campaign designed to persuade the American public not only to accept same-sex relationships as normal but to portray gay persons as society's victims and to invite straights to be their protectors. The authors' candor is quite forthright: "The campaign we outline in this book, though complex, depends centrally upon a program of unabashed propaganda, firmly grounded in long-established principles of psychology and advertising."[76]

The campaign outlined in *After the Ball* rests on the three pillars Kirk and Madsen termed desensitization, jamming, and conversion. *Desensitization* occurs when repeated exposure to something that has previously caused discomfort diminishes the discomfort – like exposure to certain animals or allergy treatments that reduce a body's sensitivity to ragweed pollen. This first move is designed to convince people that "gays are just like everybody else" and not abnormal. Like left-handed or red-haired people, they are just a minority. *Jam-*

---

[75] Marshall Kirk and Hunter Madsen, *After the Ball: How America Will Conquer Its Fear and Hatred of Gays in the 90s* (New York: Doubleday, 1989).
[76] Ibid., 26.

ming seeks to create a sense of shame in non-affirming people by making them attach their feelings of aversion and rejection based on biblical teaching to postures of bigotry, small-mindedness, and intolerance. "All normal persons feel shame when they perceive they are not thinking, feeling, or acting like one of the pack," they write. "It [a gay-normalizing ad] can depict gays experiencing horrific suffering as the direct result of homohatred – suffering of which even most bigots would be ashamed to cause."[77] Then *conversion* occurs when aversion gives way to increased likability and even affirmation of persons who cannot be seen as other than warmhearted and decent who are involved in same-sex relationships.

How this blueprint has worked can be documented from novels and movies, TV shows and their stars, athletes and musicians, or even advertisements for automobiles and vacation homes. There are very few TV sitcoms, for example, that do not have at least one comedic or heroic lead character who is openly lesbian or gay – perhaps with the show built around them. The result has been a wholesale shift of attitude toward same-sex partnerships and behaviors among young people. They have only seen gay and lesbian persons portrayed sympathetically – either as heroic in character or victimized by bigoted (usually super-religious!) villains whose behavior nobody would want to imitate.

The desired outcome of any drive to normalize same-sex coupling seems to have fulfilled the three-step process to conversion envisioned by Kirk and Madsen. "We mean conversion of the average American's emotions, mind, and will through a planned psychological attack, in the form of propaganda fed to the nation via the media."[78]

---

[77] Ibid., 150-151.
[78] Ibid., 153.

Cultural Shift #3: Changed Legal Status

When so-called "traditional moral values" are evaluated in terms of a Postmodern mindset that values personal feelings above anything that could be called an objective moral law and a culture has been systematically desensitized to its longstanding objection to same-sex intercourse, what standard is left? How does anyone determine right from wrong any longer? What should a culture generally or you as a person see as a moral norm? For most people who do not have a strong commitment to biblical ethics, the most likely arbiter of right and wrong is *law*. Civil and criminal statutes. What the lawbooks and courts decide about gambling on sports, non-medicinal use of marijuana, abortion, or same-sex intercourse settle any debate about ethical behaviors for many. "Hey, it isn't illegal!" is enough to settle the matter for them.

There has been a 180-degree turn on both the legal right to same-sex intercourse and the legal status of same-sex relationships. As recently as 1960, "sodomy" was a criminal act in all 50 states and same-sex partners applying for a marriage license at the county court clerk's office was not up for debate. Gay and lesbian persons were not allowed to serve in the military. They could not file joint tax returns with a same-sex partner or bring that partner into his or her health insurance or pension plan.

As recently as 1996 and precisely because of the social debates going on about the status of these and related issues, the United States Congress passed the Defense of Marriage Act (DOMA). DOMA specifically defined marriage as the union of one man and one woman and explicitly said "the word 'spouse' refers only to a person of the opposite sex who is a husband or a wife."[79]

---

[79] Defense of Marriage Act, H.R. 3396, 104th Cong. (1995-1996), accessed at https://www.congress.gov/bill/104th-congress/house-bill/3396/text.

In 2013, the Supreme Court struck down the law's definition of marriage as the union of one man and one woman. Then, two years later, the court followed up by striking down another provision of the law that allowed individual states to deny recognition of same-sex marriages that had been performed legally in other states. The result of these two court actions was that the right for same-sex couples to marry was declared to be a constitutional right. On December 13, 2022, President Joe Biden signed the Respect for Marriage Act into law. Its bipartisan proponents argued it was needed to guarantee that a future Supreme Court would not invalidate the 2013 and 2015 court decisions. The Respect for Marriage Act specifically mandates federal recognition for same-sex marriage.

This brief survey of only one issue from 1996 to 2022 shows how quickly public sentiment on sexual ethics has been influenced. While the focus of news reporting was on same-sex marriage over this period, moves were being made in both state and federal legislatures and courts that similarly broadened the legal recognition of LGBTQ+ persons and their rights in every arena of life in the United States. The tensions between Blue and Red policies, politicians, and states remain in place and are exploited for fund-raising and votes in countless ways.

What even many Christians seem not to appreciate is that changes in American law do not alter biblical teachings. Churches, parachurch ministries, Christian schools, and the like feel cultural pressures at various points. But the ink is still dry on what the Bible says to believers and what the church must teach and live by as an alternate community of faith in a post-Christian time. To whatever degree the laws protect LGBTQ+ persons from bigotry, unfair treatment, and violence, they are only doing what Christians should have pressed for already.

CULTURAL SHIFT #4: REINTERPRETED SCRIPTURE

Within the setting established by the three shifts just cited, the fourth was inevitable for many. Orthodox Christian teaching for 2,000 years on every continent and its long-established ethical norms for sexual behavior have been discarded in favor of the social sciences and personal experience. So biblical texts on same-sex relationships have been challenged of late by Christian leaders from what is variously called "progressive Christianity" or "new Christianity."

Figures such as Brian McLaren, Andy Stanley, and David Gushee – who gained followings from their conservative starting points – have gone on record to reject their roots for a new alternative. McLaren describes himself as "a passionate advocate for 'a new kind of Christianity' – just, generous, and working with people of all faiths for the common good." Stanley has revived the second-century Marcionite heresy already described in Chapter Four with his declaration that the twenty-first century church must "unhitch" from the Old Testament. Gushee has marked what he terms "the path to a New Christianity" that is animated by a spirit of Christian humanism.

These three have gained both attention and credibility by hammering the failings of twentieth-century fundamentalism. Pointing to the racist, sexist, and homophobic predilections of today's Evangelicalism that morphed into a hateful more-political-than-theological Christian Nationalism, they have convinced many that their rejection of those views forces them to embrace a restructured version of Christianity. And there is not enough biblical knowledge or theological sophistication in the general church population to sense where all this leads. In a word, the social sciences of Sociology and Psychology now count for more than Scripture.

A rather candid explication of all this is found in Gushee's *After Evangelicalism: The Path to a New Christianity*.[80] He begins where he must in order to reach what appear to be several predetermined conclusions about the Bible's moral instructions. He proposes a change of view about the inspiration of Scripture. He opts for what he calls "a theory of limited inspiration" within which "*some scriptural texts consistently demonstrate that they are inspired by God because they prove so useful in Christian experience for drawing people to Jesus and his way.*"[81] This "limited" view permits him to put other sources of spiritual guidance on par with the Bible for "discerning truth." Thus, we should "do some fresh thinking about other ways of knowing – indeed, other ways of hearing God address us. These include tradition, science, reason, experience, intuition, community, and relationships."[82]

The notion of hearing God's voice from sources beyond Scripture has been the springboard for many a challenge to Christian orthodoxy. More than once have I been told by someone in conversation that "God spoke to me and said . . ." things ranging from her right to take a lover because of her insensitive husband to a bizarre new meaning (and content!) for the bread and wine of the Lord's Supper. That one has heard God's voice through psychology, personal experience, intuition, or a lover allows what once might have been called "Christian faith and morals" to be "whatever I choose to believe and do." As Ron Highfield has noted:

> Hence the church's traditional teaching that the Bible alone is the ultimate norm of Christian faith and morals must be rejected. To defend their progressive views, progressives reinterpret, correct, reject, or even condemn the teaching of Scripture. God's "voice" in personal experience, political movements, culture,

---

[80] David P. Gushee, *After Evangelicalism: The Path to a New Christianity* (Louisville: Westminster John Knox Press, 2020).
[81] Ibid., 32. Note: italics for emphasis are in the original text.
[82] Ibid., 40-41.

and psychology in certain cases trumps Scripture. Apparently the "progress" of progressive Christianity depends on a constant flow of new divine revelations. It should not escape notice that these new revelations track almost perfectly, albeit a few months behind, with advances in secular culture and politics.[83]

Highfield also provides a helpful distinction between what it is to "interpret" versus "reinterpret" a biblical text. The legitimate task of literate Bible students is to interpret the original language and historical setting of a text in order "to unite the mind of the listener with the original meaning of the text along with its full implications and applications." On the other hand, to reinterpret "usually means not merely to challenge older, established interpretations but to read an alien meaning into the text with as much plausibility as one can create. It is to hijack the accrued authority of a text and place it in service of a meaning more acceptable to the interpreter."[84]

Gushee – who bills himself as a "scholar" in the field of "Christian ethics" – is so disoriented in his search for a new Christianity that he seems to have determined that psychology trumps Scripture. Thus he writes of the "need to adjust faith to the legitimate discoveries of science."[85] The specific "legitimate discoveries" he references are the "sheer facticity of homosexuality," the change of position on same-sex relationships in the 1970s by "every major professional association of psychologists and sexologists," and his own personal experience with LGBTQ+ persons. "What needed to change was not gay and lesbian people," he now affirms, "but the cultural worldviews that stigmatized and harmed them."[86]

With due respect for my friends who do responsible work in psychology and counseling and Gushee's view of their professional

---

[83] Ron Highfield, "A New Christianity? A Post-Evangelical Progressive Vision (Part 1)," accessed at https://ifaqtheology.com/2022/11/07/a-new-christianity-a-post-evangelical-progressive-vision-part-1.
[84] Ibid.
[85] Gushee, *After Evangelicalism*, 129.
[86] Ibid.

associations, that a given percentage of the population is gay or that the American Psychiatric Association and American Psychological Association have reclassified same-sex behavior from "mental disorder" to "alternative lifestyle" says nothing about its moral classification. Statistics about the number of people who self-identify as trans, intersex, lesbian, pansexual, gay, or queer is math, not morality. Math describes what *is* in terms of counting and listing; morality prescribes what *ought to be* in terms of approval and propriety. For Christians, the source of moral knowledge is not counting noses but biblical truth.

Referring to the matter of its "statistical incidence" (i.e., Gushee's "facticity"), Richard Hays makes a point of saying "that would not settle the *normative* issue; it is impossible to argue simply from an 'is' to an 'ought.' If Paul were shown the poll results, he would reply sadly, 'Indeed, the power of sin is rampant in the world.'"[87]

CULTURAL SHIFT #5: "BUT IT'S SOMEONE I LOVE!"

At first glance, what I am calling a fifth cultural shift may not seem to be anything new to you. And you could be correct. I am not denying for a moment that human beings across the centuries – including me in this one – are inclined to make allowances for or simply excuse the behaviors of the people we love. Because she is my friend, I "understand" her bad temper. Because we've been friends since college days, I can make allowances for his "drinking a bit too much." Surely all of us are tempted to do that sort of thing for close family members. I have watched any number of people I know change their views on LGBTQ+ behaviors because it was his sister, her brother, or their child who "outed herself" as lesbian or decided to "transition" to the opposite sex or announced his intention to marry another man.

---

[87] Hays, *Moral Vision of the New Testament*, 398.

But there has been an even more significant cultural shift in the name of love. In the twenty-first century, individuals not only turn a blind eye to things done by someone they love but a whole culture has been led to think that anything done in the name of love cannot be judged morally wrong. For example, when President Biden signed the Respect for Marriage Act into law on December 13, 2022, he said this of the bipartisan bill Congress had passed: "Republicans and Democrats can work together to secure the fundamental right of Americans to marry the person they love."[88]

Does anyone *really* believe a person should be free to marry anyone he or she loves? His neighbor and best friend's wife? Her tenth-grade algebra student? His sister? "Why shouldn't two people in love be granted the right to get married?" is the defense of polygamy and polyandry. Moral rights and limitations derive from ethical principles that are defensible from moral reasoning. When reason or – for Christians at least – biblical teaching is allowed to be replaced by romantic feelings, practically any relationship scenario seems to be acceptable.

Eve Tushnet is Jewish by birth. She is single. She self-identifies as lesbian. Because of the teaching of her church and what she has come to believe the Bible teaches about the nature of marriage and its interconnected prohibition of same-sex relationships, however, she lives a celibate life – after living in a same-sex partnership herself for several years prior to her conversion. She writes:

> One of the frightening aspects of loving somebody is the way that love can seem to offer unique access not only to pleasure but to truth. Love of another person – not only romantic love, but familial love and deep friendship as well – promises or threatens to reshape us completely. It can become the lens through which we see the world.[89]

---

[88] Michael D. Shear, "Biden Signs Bill to Protect Same-Sex Marriage Rights," *New York Times*, Dec 20, 2022, accessed at https://www.nytimes.com/2022/12/13/us/politics/biden-same-sex-marriage-bill.html?searchResultPosition=1.

[89] Eve Tushnet, "Homosexuality & the Church: A Second View," *Commonweal*, June 11, 2007, accessed at https://www.commonwealmagazine.org/print/36052.

Tushnet did not create the cultural climate that had taught her to think that love sets aside all other factors. Romantic feelings that draw human beings to one another are built into us by the Creator. They draw us out of our insular selves to be part of the relational community that is humanity. In a narrower sense, they attract us to and focus our attention on particular individuals with whom we come to be "in love" and whose attention, affection, and intimate life connections we want to share. In the brokenness that is common to our race, however, some women are drawn to and come to be "in love" with men who exploit and abuse them. Some men "fall in love" with women who wind up breaking faith with them and having affairs. With all the confusion that surrounds romantic love, how can we be shocked that some people wind up "in love" with someone of the same sex?

In spite of a Beatles' song that says "Love is all you need, love," you likely know it can put you in situations that demand making hard choices. In Tushnet's case, it came down to a choice between a partner she loved romantically and the Christ she was coming to love by faith. She is not the first or last person to face such a dilemma. Jesus said it would happen: "If anyone comes to me and does not hate father and mother, wife and children, brothers and sisters – yes, even their own life – such a person cannot be my disciple" (Luke 14:26). He knew that some of his would-be followers would have to make terribly hard choices to be his disciple. Our generation has found a way to dismiss this tough demand rather than have to accept it.

The key to resolving the dilemma, of course, is neither to deny the power of romantic human love nor to minimize the demands of true discipleship. It is to realize that love for God is more fundamental and precious than love for family, friends, nation, or even life itself. "We should seek to reconcile love of God and love of others whenever they appear to conflict," Tushnet continues. "But we can't simply assume that such a conflict never exists – or that, if a conflict seems to arise, God couldn't possibly be asking us to sacrifice a human relationship."

Jesus used the metaphors of gouging out an eye or cutting off a hand to help his disciples understand just how costly discipleship could be (Matt 5:29-30). It is not insignificant that he was discussing personal relationships when he used that language. When power, money, or a human relationship takes priority over someone's love for and devotion to God, it becomes his or her god and turns the person into what the Bible calls an idolator. Perhaps that is precisely why Paul used male-with-male and female-with-female love as examples of what happens when a culture exchanges the truth it can know about God for an idol.

Conclusion

But what if there is a sense in which love not only *does* conquer all but *should* do so? What if one's love for God is greater than his love for money, her love of achievement, or their romantic love for someone who is forbidden to them by their love for God? Surely this possibility is what Jesus was talking about when he said – in the language of hyperbole already quoted above – that some people would have to "hate" their closest loves and even their own lives in order to follow him. This was a theme he returned to more than once in his teaching (cf. Matt 10:37; John 12:25).

From ancient times until Jesus returns, people find it is necessary to make choices. Some have had to make the sort of extreme choice of friend, family member, or lover for the sake of their love of God. We could pray that love for God would "conquer all" that has the potential to turn us away from him.

6

Questions for Reflection

THINK ABOUT...
THE CULTURAL CONTEXT OF YOUR LIFE

Serious Question: "Do you think fish know they are in water?" *Application:* Human beings are as immersed in culture as fish are in water. Likewise, we can assess ourselves, others, and God only from within our cultural context. Most accept the culture to which they are born without questioning it. *Challenge:* Without the "anchor points" of a biblical worldview, Christians do not know how to critique, live within, and address our culture.

EXPLORE...
COLOSSIANS 3:1-14

Some basic anchor points of a Christian worldview are identified in this text. To whom do Christians look for the meaning of life? What is the ultimate hope for those who find their life direction in Christ? To find newness in Christ, what must happen to the old practices and habits of the world's culture? What metaphor does Paul use to describe the transition from one culture to another in these verses?

PRACTICE...
INFORMED INTERPRETATION OF THE BIBLE

1. Our culture's view of sexual permissiveness has changed rapidly. Why do you think mainline churches have followed the cultural drift so uncritically? Does the UMC's history teach us anything helpful here?

2. Did you know the term "Moralistic Therapeutic Deism" before reading Chapter Six? Does the Smith-Denton term make sense to you?

3. Define in your words the three distorted ethical principles discussed in the chapter.

4. Why is it important to understand the cultural shifts discussed here? Can you name specific things you witness that illustrate them? Are there others you would add to the five listed here?

5. A different take on the love-conquers-all theme closes out the chapter. What are your thoughts on it?

6. What is your most important takeaway from Chapter Six?

*The Afterword to this book speaks to the issue of
loving, serving, and helping people deal with
same-sex attraction and related issues.
A gay man who now is living a chaste life suggests
several ways this might be done. Among those
suggestions, his one deserves special notice.*
The Ink Is Dry *has been an attempt to do
what he has advised.*

The ministries that have helped me most *take the risk of speaking up about same-sex attraction.* For a congregation to even broach the topic of homosexuality is dangerous right now, because it's almost guaranteed to offend dozens of people on every "side" and to cause a firestorm. But what if Christians stay silent? What if we never preach a sermon on this, or lead a Bible study on it, or mention it in a prayer group? . . .

The ministries that have helped me venture to say something about how I might live my life, how I might go about giving and receiving love. The times when a Christian friend or priest has offered me some concrete, hopeful possibility of how I might shape my life – those have been lifelines for me. But they have required my friends to take the risk of speaking up and of committing themselves to learning along with me.

Another feature of the ministries that have helped me most is their *engaging Scripture and Christian theology in a deep, rigorous way.* We same-sex attracted folks do not have the luxury of remaining neutral on "the issue." Since we must make concrete choices about how to "glorify God in our bodies" (1 Corinthians 6:20), many of us crave deep, searching engagement with Scripture and Christian theology. We are impatient with hasty arguments and shallow scriptural reasoning. We are frustrated when our fellow Christians want to slap a quick answer on our questions. . . .

Clearly, theology matters. Serious, sustained reading of Scripture is vital to those of us who are trying to figure out what to do with our baptized bodies. We need ministries that recognize this.

Wesley Hill, "The Long Defeat," The Institute of Faith
and Learning at Baylor University (online), 26-28.
Accessed at https://www.baylor.edu/content/services/
document.php/277021.pdf%20Feb%2019.

> *Those who have rightly understood
> the mystery of the gospel will
> exert themselves to live rightly.*
>
> – Ulrich Zwingli

AFTERWORD

The great need of every human being is not sex, but intimacy.

Please! Before reading further, go back and read the sentence above. It is critical to the thesis of this book, central to a well-formed theory of human development, and at the heart of what the Bible says about the meaning of human life.

It is an empirical fact that human beings can live without sex, but we die without love. Multiple studies have been done of high mortality rates among infants and small children who "fail to flourish" or die because of a lack of simple human contact – being held, fed, rocked, and talked to by a real person. At the other end of the age spectrum, both scholarly studies and articles in the popular press document the effects of loneliness in elderly people. Humans need each other in order to be truly and fully human.

The most bewildered people along the age spectrum are teenagers. And their bewilderment is manifesting itself in mental health problems that make frequent and frightening headlines.

In 2020, 16% of U.S. kids ages 12 to 17 had anxiety, depression, or both, a roughly 33% increase since 2016, according to an analysis by health-policy research group Kaiser Family Foundation (KFF). The following year, 42% of U.S. high school students said they felt persistently sad or hopeless, 29% reported experiencing poor mental health, 22% had seriously considered suicide, and 10% had attempted suicide, according to the U.S. Centers for Disease Control and Prevention (CDC).[90]

For gay activists such as Matthew Vines, of course, the poor mental health of many of these young people likely traces – in the language of his website – to something other than TikTok, Covid-19, and climate change. "Church teachings that condemn same-sex relationships and transgender people cause serious harm in the lives of LGBTQ Christians."[91]

If Modernity created the myth of human agents as cogs within machines who find their greatest dignity within some monolithic scheme of national or political, ideological or corporate, social or family system, Postmodernity has revolted against all system-building. Instead, it has opted for unfettered human interaction that rejects the boundaries drawn by any authority or organization that would seek to deny their exchanges. So the Kinsey-based and culturally endorsed personal freedom to "love whomever you will" has generated the false reckoning that having sex with someone is being loved and loving. The promise of the 1960s that throwing off the old rules and inhibitions would be the dawning of a whole new world of delight in human experience has failed. Instead, it has spawned a worldview that has confused practically all of Western civilization about sex and created countless anxieties on the subject for people of all ages. And churches have not been notably helpful with them. In fact, there is good evidence that some well-known Christian spokesmen have contributed to making the problem worse.

---

[90] Jamie Ducharme, "'We're in a New World': American Teenagers on Mental Health and How to Cope," *Time*, Oct 10, 2023, accessed at https://time.com/6320195/us-teen-mental-health-photos.

[91] "The Problem," *The Reformation Project* website, accessed at https://reformationproject.org.

Afterword

AN ALTERNATIVE VISION FOR LIVING

This is not the first time in history that the church has been called to step to the front to present an alternative vision of human flourishing. That "alternative vision" will not come from some form of full-frontal assault on our culture – a new political party, lobbying for new laws (or the return of old ones), or marching in the streets. It will come from the church being the church and modeling the safety, inclusion, and support of God's family of redeemed people who live by biblical faith. There will be the sort of magnetic draw to that community that has been witnessed historically when the church lives as *a Christ-centered community of acceptance, accountability, and nurture where gradual spiritual transformation takes place over time.* Within such a community, there is love. There is a true sense of belonging. There is intergenerational intimacy among males and females, marrieds and singles.

Luke paints a verbal picture of how this sort of *koinonia* – a Greek word indicating partnership, association, shareholding – worked in the church's earliest days at Acts 2:42-47. They ate together, prayed together, and shared their resources. They were generous beyond their own members and established a reputation for being kind even to their enemies and persecutors. In the second century, a Greek philosopher named Aristides reported to Emperor Hadrian about the Christians and wrote:

> They love one another; the widows' needs are not ignored, and they rescue the orphan from the person who does him violence. He who has gives to him who has not, ungrudgingly and without boasting. . . . If they hear of any of their number who are imprisoned or oppressed for the name of the Messiah, they all provide for his needs, and if it is possible to redeem him, they set him free.[92]

---

[92] *Apology of Aristides.* 15.

And you have surely come across the frequently quoted words of Tertullian (*ca.* 160-220) who, commenting on what the pagans were saying about his fellow-Christians, offered this: "'Look,' they say, 'how they love one another' (for they themselves hate one another); 'and how they are ready to die for each other' (for they themselves are readier to kill each other)."[93] This model of the church as a community of loving presence will be part of any local church's effective ministry to persons dealing with any number of issues related to sexuality.

Whether a tempted (or promiscuous) young person, a teenager with gender dysphoria (or already trans), a young adult who is same-sex oriented (or active), a member who "comes out" as gay or lesbian, an opposite-sex couple on the brink of divorce, or a straight couple trying to help a child or relative dealing with one of these issues, *churches need to be safe places where members can confide rather than conceal in order to seek healing.* Surely this is an obvious application of New Testament texts such as these:

> If someone falls into sin, forgivingly restore him, saving your critical comments for yourself. *You* might be needing forgiveness before the day's out. Stoop down and reach out to those who are oppressed. Share their burdens, and so complete Christ's law. If you think you are too good for that, you are badly deceived (Gal 6:1-2 MSG).
>
> Confess your sins to each other and pray for each other so that you may be healed. The earnest prayer of a righteous person has great power and produces wonderful results (Jas 5:16 NLT).

That these two epistles are generally believed to be the very earliest books of our New Testament to be written may well indicate the need Jewish believers had to show patience and love to their Gentile brothers and sisters who were still so fresh from their pagan backgrounds.

---

93 *Apologeticus.* 39. 7.

Afterword

In our own time, think of the way many churches have learned to deal with alcohol and drug addiction. Twelve-step groups meet on their properties. Some of those groups are simply given space for meetings that are led by non-members of those churches or even non-Christians. The problems associated with chemical addiction are so varied and deep that church members are eager to provide encouragement for anyone in their larger communities who are taking steps to address them. In other churches, similar support groups meet during Sunday School hours and forego the anonymity of traditional Alcoholics Anonymous or Narcotics Anonymous groups.

Why should we be reluctant to offer the same help to persons dealing with an even more powerful "addiction" – the relationship addictions that are known to develop from or else to lead to sexual behaviors that violate biblical norms? Think that sort of thing could never work? Dr. Roy Hamley and I announced the formation of such a group for persons with AIDS (acquired immunodeficiency syndrome) in the early 1980s – when the medical establishment was trying to understand this new disease that we more often hear of today as HIV (human immunodeficiency virus) infection.

Dr. Hamley was an elder of the church I was serving at the time, and the project had the support of the full shepherding body of the church. We had no more than formed the first group until there needed to be two. Members of the larger church body formed two seven-member Care Teams in conjunction with a Nashville group that served the gay community. These Care Teams committed to seeing terminal AIDS patients through the final months of their lives by taking them to physician appointments, helping them shop for groceries or shopping for them, providing companionship through lonely days, and simply being available as friends. I did a number of funerals for persons who died of the disease – including at least one where Christian members of the deceased person's family announced in their home church the man had died of cancer. I became an AIDS Educator for the American Red Cross. Dr. Hamley and his wife, Mary, counseled and comforted more people than I could count.

The point of this history is not to make Roy, Mary, or me "look good" or to boast of "what good people we are." It is to say that churches are mistaken to think that people will not accept loving help from Christians who believe and teach that alcoholism, drug addiction, or sex outside a covenanted male-female marriage is outside God's will. Our conviction about those activities need not be a stick with which we threaten or bludgeon people. (By the way, several other support and recovery groups were going on during that same period in that church – at least one of which dealt with men struggling with pornography, two with female survivors of childhood sexual abuse, and one with sexual addiction.) People can face both harms done to them and the harms they are doing to themselves and others when given the opportunity to do so in a context of supportive love. Shaming and belittling only drive people who need and would otherwise welcome help to hide their problems.

With regard to men and women who are single – whether by circumstance, choice, or self-denial – the church simply must do more to incorporate them into its life. Marriage is neither the pinnacle of human life nor a guarantee of sexual fulfillment. Neither is sexual partnership nor parenthood a fundamental right each person can claim. Christ's call to faithful discipleship entails the promise of eternal life, not sexual gratification.

BACK TO THE ISSUE OF IDOLATRY

Chapter 1 of this book promised to come back to the subject of *idolatry* and its claimed link to same-sex behaviors in Romans 1. Not only in Paul's letters, but from the golden calf at Mount Sinai through the prophets of the Old Testament and into John's record of the Revelation he received from Jesus, idolatry is the root sin that undergirds all human anguish.

All this means that the subject matter of this book is not a marginal topic. It isn't one about which we can "just agree to disagree" – and go our separate ways. Do Christians really have the option to behave as people of the world? Can we persist in sin without repenting and not damage both our personal faith and the community of believers the New Testament calls the church? Paul posed this question long ago – and answered it by the Spirit of God.

> What shall we say, then? Shall we go on sinning so that grace may increase? By no means! We are those who have died to sin; how can we live in it any longer? . . . Therefore do not let sin reign in your mortal body so that you obey its evil desires. Do not offer any part of yourself to sin as an instrument of wickedness, but rather offer yourselves to God as those who have been brought from death to life; and offer every part of yourself to him as an instrument of righteousness (Rom 6:1-2, 12-13).

Could language be clearer? One school of thought about a believer's security in Christ would say that anyone who professed faith in Jesus as Lord and then persists in unrepented sin simply was never saved to begin with. Another says that saved persons who turn their back on Jesus by living in unrepented sin can fall from grace and be lost. In either case, what is inconceivable is that Christians would argue that it is possible to believe, teach, and live impenitently as a fornicator, adulterer, or sexually active lesbian or gay person to the glory of God! The words of Jesus break through at this point with power: "Anyone who sets aside one of the least of these commands and teaches others accordingly will be called least in the kingdom of heaven" (Matt 5:19).

Over against the homophobic rantings of some that "God Hates Queers," the message of the church I want to be part of offers redemption from sin – *all* sin. If Paul can say that "neither the sexually immoral nor idolators nor adulterers nor men who have sex with men" will inherit and share the blessings of the kingdom of God, he also says the same thing about others; "neither thieves nor the greedy nor drunkards nor slanderers nor swindlers will inherit the kingdom of God" (1 Cor 6:9-10). The point here is that sexual sin is one category of wrong behavior among many others. *And Christ's message of redemptive grace reaches to all who are in bondage to sins of whatever nature.*

The church is not commissioned to announce or practice hatred toward lesbians or greedy people, alcoholics or thieves, transgendered persons or mudslinging politicians. Instead, a faithful community of Christ-followers serves as a living witness to sexual purity and generosity, sobriety and responsibility, personal integrity and self-restraint. *As sinners in pursuit of holiness, penitent people in process of transformation invite rather than attack those who may be precisely where we were at one time in our own journeys.*

In the verse that follows the list just cited and in which Paul names various persons who will not receive the blessings of God's reign on Earth, the apostle adds this: "And that is what some of you were. But you were washed, you were sanctified, you were justified in the name of the Lord Jesus Christ and by the Spirit of our God" (1 Cor 6:11). This is why the gospel is "good news." In God's presence with us through Jesus of Nazareth, there is not only pardon but also renewal. By the indwelling Spirit, there is strength to face temptations successfully.

In that same first-century church Paul wrote to in Corinth, a man who persisted in an incestuous self-indulgence was censured by Paul and the Christians instructed by the apostle to exclude him from their fellowship (cf. 1 Cor 5:1-8). While Paul made it clear that the church had no right or power to set the standards for Corinth, Scripture establishes the norms for Christ's church. While Christians must be careful not to judge those outside our own number, we must teach and apply biblical teaching among our own (cf. 1 Cor 5:9-13).

If we take the Pauline language seriously enough that we regard it as Spirit-guided instruction, persons who willingly engage in same-sex practices are thereby barred from the Kingdom of God. Put another way, their choice to act out their sexual impulses with persons of the same sex is a choice not to live under God's reign and within his revealed will. By that choice, they also forgo the privilege of participating in the communion of believers who are the present expression of the Kingdom of God. The church is forbidden to give its fellowship and approval to anyone involved in habitual and unrepented behavior of whatever sort. Just as the incestuous man in the Corinthian church was to be disciplined on apostolic authority, so must churches in our time and place exclude from their fellowship any brother or sister who is involved in blatant rebellion against biblical instruction.

Harsh as that language sounds to an anything-goes culture, the purpose of such an action is not only for the sake of the church's integrity within a *laissez-faire* moral environment such as Corinth or contemporary North America but also for the rescue of a soul in jeopardy. It is the spiritual well-being of that person that is, in fact, the critical goal of this process. That is why so extreme an action as the severing of fellowship with a Christian brother or sister is allowed only at the end of a process of teaching and pleading (cf. Matt 18:15-18) – teaching and pleading that is gentle and willing to help that person regain his or her footing.

Interestingly, our 2 Corinthians points to the success of the discipline process ordered by the apostle in his earlier letter. The discipline of his having been excluded from the church's fellowship had the desired effect of bringing him to his senses. He came to view what he had done in the light of Christ's righteousness, embraced a sense of godly sorrow for his behavior, and was brought back into the Christian community. Rather than keep him at arm's length and extend his discipline, Paul used his authority as an apostle to order his readmittance. "You ought to forgive and comfort him, so that he will not be overwhelmed by excessive sorrow," he wrote. "I urge you, therefore, to reaffirm your love for him" (2 Cor 2:7-8). Both the rebuke and the reception back into the church were acts of love. Churches that follow a biblical model in our time must not only stand resolutely for biblical sexual ethics but equally for a gentle, instructive, and restorative method of Christian love in dealing with those whose lives are off track.

Conclusion

Only if idolatry is of no consequence to faith can we ignore the various issues in Scripture that relate to human sexual behaviors. Only if love ceases to be the foundation of Christian relationships can we be abusive in tone and manner with persons who have been caught up in sexual sin.

In a world where there was no such thing as sin, perhaps we would not cry out for God's grace or the compassion of his children. In the world we have and in which sin reigns, however, the gospel demands that the truth be spoken, repentance be real, grace be received, and Christ's compassion be allowed to bring people healing and health. Only in that sort of Christian community can discipleship thrive and people grow into the likeness of Christ.

That human life is essentially a choice between doing things "my way" versus doing them "God's way" is a theme that runs through the entire Bible.

Afterword

Psalm 1 celebrates the God-fearing soul who delights in the Word of God and flourishes spiritually. That person is like a tree whose roots are nourished by life-giving streams. By contrast, the one whose life leads to destruction fails to flourish by virtue of depending on self rather than God. In his Sermon on the Mount, Jesus makes the same point in his Parable of the Two Builders. One of them built on the sand of his own insights and the other on the solid rock of hearing his teachings and putting them into practice (Matt 7:24-27). And Paul builds a great deal of his letter to the church at Rome around the contrast between a life that focuses on selfish pleasures versus the one that follows the path marked by the Holy Spirit (Rom 8:5-8).

What David, Jesus, and Paul taught in ancient times is still true today. May God give us ears willing to hear and hearts eager to obey.

INDEX OF SCRIPTURES

Genesis 43-61, 87-88, 97-99, 105, 117-118, 141-142
1:27   48, 52, 88, 118
1:28   42, 52, 53, 141
2:7   48, 49(fn)
2:18   51-53, 118
2:20   51
2:22   88
2:23   48, 88
2:24   52(3), 88
2:25   88
3:8   97
3:24   98(2)
6:6   85
13:13   91
15:13-16 85
18:20   91
18:23   91
19:4-5 91
19:30-38 91

Exodus
19:6   10
34:6-7 83-84

Leviticus 96-103
11:44-45 10, 86
18   95-96, 100
18:22   96, 100, 127
18:24-27 85, 96
18:26   96, 100
19:2   10, 68
20:7   10
20:13   96, 100, 127
20:26   10
21:8   10
26:12   97
27:13   98

Deuteronomy
15:7-11 25
19:15-19 28
20:10   85
28:15ff 84

Joshua
2   85

Judges
17:6   139
21:25   139

Psalms
1   170

Proverbs
14:12   145

Song of Solomon 53

Isaiah
45:19   28
49:6   30
54:5   47
54:7-8 84(2)

Jeremiah
29:5-7 30
31:3   84
31:31-32 47
32:34-35 84

Lamentations 84

Ezekiel 94
16:49-50 92, 95
16:51   95
22:11   96

33:11   129
33:26   96

Daniel
1:3-5   30
1:18-21 30

Habakkuk
2:14   108

Matthew
5:17-19 39, 82, 87, 111, 167
5:21-48 82, 87
5:29-30 157
6:33   144
7:15-20 59
7:24-27 171
10:37   157
13:45-46 37
15:9   39
15:19   110
18:15-18 169
19:1-9 47, 62, 88, 111, 142
19:12   60
19:14   110
25:31-46 25
28:19   122

Mark
7:17-23 82, 110

Luke
2:36-37 60
10:25-37 79
14:26   156
24:37-39 92

John
1:17	*27, 29*
8:1ff	*22, 28-29*
8:44	*113*
12:25	*157*

Acts
2:42-47	*163*
17	*121*
20:32	*19*
21:39	*111*

Romans
1:18-32	*113, 117(fn), 125*
1:20	*118, 126*
1:22-32	*115, 124-125*
6:1-2	*167*
6:12-13	*167*
8:5-8	*171*
11:24	*119*
15:4	*87, 104*

1 Corinthians
5:1-11	*126, 169(2)*
5:3	*112*
5:9-13	*32-33, 169*
6:9-10	*64, 127, 168*
6:11	*77, 129, 131, 168*
6:19-20	*50, 75, 127(2), 139*
7:25-28	*60*
10:11	*87*
11:14-15	*120-121*
14:37	*112*
15:35ff	*49*

2 Corinthians
2:7-8	*170*
10:7	*112*
13:14	*122*

Galatians
2:20	*37*
5:13-26	*77*
6:1-2	*164*

Ephesians
2:1-10	*77*
5:21-23	*47, 76*

Philippians
3:7-8	*38*

Colossians 36-37
2:8	*36*
2:20-23	*36*
3:1-4	*37*
3:1-17	*77, 159*

3:10	*117*
3:5-4:6	*39*

Hebrews
1:1-2	*86*
1:14	*92*
13:4	*12, 13(2), 75*
13:8	*86*

James
1:17	*86*
2:14-16	*25*
2:26	*49*
5:16	*164*

1 Peter 41-42
1:15-16	*68*
2:11-17	*41*
2:18-25	*130*

2 Peter
2:6-7	*92-94*

Jude
7	*91-94*

Revelation
19:1-4	*47*
21:3	*109*

INDEX OF PERSONS & SUBJECTS

AA/Alcoholics Anonymous, 165
abortion, 22, 137, 149
abuse, sexual, 16, 44, 45, 84, 128, 130, 156, 166
abusive language toward gay/lesbian persons, 29-30
Adam and Eve, 51-54, 63, 69, 98
adam (Hebrew for "human"), 50
adultery, 29, 46, 59, 82, 87-88, 100, 119, 140
After the Ball (book), 26, 147
"affirming" views/writers, 11, 27, 32, 45, 59, 68, 88-89, 94, 99, 110, 122, 123, 125, 124
Aphrodite, 70
Aristotle, 78, 119
arsenokoitēs/arsenokoitai, 127-128
Athens, 70, 71, 73, 78, 121, 123

bad-fruit argument (Vines), 57-59
bestiality, 11, 13, 85, 88, 89, 98, 100, 110, 111
Bible
   authority, 14, 16, 24, 27, 28, 33, 46, 48, 62, 86, 104-105, 107, 112, 136, 138, 140, 145, 150
   mishandling, 11, 27, 32, 45, 60, 62, 67, 80, 81, 85, 89, 90-96, 101, 106, 135, 152, 153
   no affirmative case for same-sex union, 11, 75, 106
   superior to experience, 136, 139, 145, 152-156
bigot/bigotry, 27, 54, 137, 145, 148, 150
Boeotian "yoke-mates", 71, 78
Boswell, John, 73-74, 99

castration, 60, 121
celibacy
   distinguished from purity, 76
chastity, 10, 42, 76, 112, 138
church
   community for spiritual support, 39, 40, 162-183
   duty to biblical truth, 29, 154
   historic view of sexual behaviors, 77, 111
   relationship to the state, 16, 30-31, 101, 136, 140, 149
church discipline, 169-170
Christian Nationalism, 30, 102, 137-138, 151
civil law and Christian ethics, 11, 30-31, 101, 140

Corinth, 32, 102, 112-113, 126-131, 139, 168-169
Cybele, cult of, 73, 78, 121

disciple/discipleship, 157, 166, 170

erastēs, 45
Eve, See Adam and Eve
Ezekiel, See Index of Scriptures

fate, 123-124
Favale, Abigail, 50-51
feelings and moral truth, 34, 142-143, 145, 149, 155-156
fluidity, sex/gender, 50, 56
fornication, 76, 110, 119

gender-affirming care, 32, 132
   scientific reservation, 32, 57-58
gender dysphoria, 22, 32, 56-59, 63, 132, 164
Genesis, Ch 2 (43-61), 87-88
   "image of God," 15, 29, 46, 48, 50-52, 67, 98, 107, 117-118
   creation story, 42, 60, 97-98
   normative for marriage, 88, 102-103, 117, 141-142, 154
   sexual differentiation, 46-47, 87-88, 118
Gushee, David, 10, 11, 45fn, 89, 122, 151
   "limited" inspiration, view of Bible's, 152-154

hair
   cephalic (head), 55, 120-121
   facial (beard), 70, 72
Harper, Kyle, 74, 120
Hays, Richard, 118, 154
Highfield, Ron, 152-153
Hill, Wesley, 160
Holiness Code, 48, 96, 99-105, 111, 115, 127
Holland, Tom, 20, 113
Holy Spirit, 33, 39, 40, 49, 76
   indwelling presence, 168
   source of moral strength, 35, 39
   source of spiritual life, 33, 171
homophobia, 15, 151
   Christian duty to reject, 15, 29-30, 167
homosexual/homosexuality, 27, 89, 95, 118, 119fn, 122, 134

Index of Persons & Subjects

change of perspective in recent years, 27, 146, 153
orientation vs behaviors, 117fn,
orientation in Greek thought, 123
use of terminology in this book, 34, 44fn, 123
Hubbard, Thomas, 123

idolatry, 24, 33, 100, 116, 166
ancient cultures, 84-85, 99
dehumanizing effect, 44, 68, 114
link to sexual sin, 115, 166, 170
variety of forms, 24, 96, 115
incest, 13, 47, 85, 88, 91, 99, 111, 125, 131, 140, 168-169
intimacy, 53-54, 75, 141, 161, 163
ish/ishah, 52

Jesus, 47, 109, 156, 167, 170
life as single (unmarried) person, 60
teaching on same-sex relationships, 17, 86-88, 98, 109-111, 112, 131, 142
teaching on sexual purity, 28-29, 82, 88
Jews/Judaism (on same-sex relationships), 87, 117
Johnson, Luke Timothy, 106
judging, 33, 140, 155
appropriate moral judgments, 12
inappropriate personal judgments, 39, 102, 168

kata physin, 118-119
Keen, Karen, 88-89, 94
Keller, Tim, 24-26, 38, 42
Kirk, Marshall, See *After the Ball* (book), 26, 147
koinonia, 163

law, See civil law and Christian ethics
lesbian/lesbianism, 9, 15, 17-18, 29, 31, 110, 115, 119, 122, 124, 128, 133, 145-149, 153-155, 164, 167-168
loneliness, 53, 161
nature of Adam's, 53
psychological/emotional, 54, 161
love, 16, 70, 156, 161, 163, 170
God's, Ch 1 (21-42), 20, 76, 83-85, 107-108, 136
love and truth, 152-153, 155, 157
love in friendship relations, 154, 161

love for God, 76-77, 95, 97, 108, 157
love for LGBTQ+ persons, 29, 40, 85
married love, 53, 141-142
misdirected love, 53, 155

McKnight, Scot, 64, 80
Madsen, Hunter, See *After the Ball* (book)
malakos/malakoi, 127-128
marriage, 9, 12, 24-26, 61
    heterosexual as normative, 10, 12, 46-48, 69, 75-77, 88, 142
    protected by biblical restrictions, 13, 35, 88, 111, 129
    redefinition, 31, 47, 133-134, 145, 149-150, 155
    same-sex, 11, 13, 48, 69-74
    same-sex marriage in church fathers, 119
moral law
    how derived, 10, 86, 100-101, 113, 136
    relation to ceremonial law, 99, 101
Moralistic Therapeutic Deism, 135-138, 160

nature, See *kata physin, para physin*
orientation, sexual, 12, 40, 45fn, 115, 122-124
    vs behaviors, 34, 139

paiderastēs/paiderastein, 45fn
para physin, 118-120
passivity, male sexual, 127
Paul, 32, 36-37, 73-74, 139, 166-171
    life as single (unmarried) person, 60
    relationship of Christians to OT, 82-83, 87, 96, 102-103, 104
    view of same-sex behaviors, 77, 86, 111-129, 130-131,
pedophilia, 16, 45, 68, 77, 110
Peter, 17, 66, 73, 83
    ethical instruction, 41, 130
    reference to Sodom in 2 Peter, 92, 94
Plato, 49, 78, 80
    on training the morals of the young, 69-70
    same-sex coupling in the *Symposium*, 70-71, 78
    concept of sexual orientation, 123
porneiai, 110
Postmodernism, 142-145, 149, 162
procreation, See reproduction

prostitute/prostitution, 12, 13, 16, 45, 46, 59, 68, 77, 112, 119, 125, 127-128
purity, sexual, See celibacy

repentance, 35, 84-85, 129, 170
reproduction, 12, 43, 46, 52-54, 103, 141
Roman/Rome, 25, 38, 113, 121
    chart of LGBTQ+ persons, 78
    same-sex marriages, 72-74, 78
    sexual ethics, 68, 80, 112, 64
Romans, Epistle to the, 96, 113-126

Sacred Band of Thebes, 71-72, 78, 80, 126
same-sex partnerships, 10
    known in antiquity, 13, 45, 68-74, 75, 77, 78, 123, 125
    legalization in U.S., 149-150, 155
    recent shift in attitude about, 22, 133-134, 145-148
Scripture, See Bible
single life, 40, 60, 112, 163
slaves/slavery, 51, 68, 97
    exploited by sexual abuse, 13, 16, 45, 112, 128
Sodom, 89-96, 105
sodomy, 11, 89, 149
spectrum theory of sexual identity, 50, 56
Stanley, Andy, 151
state, See church, relationship to state
Symposium (Plato's), 70-71, 80

Thebes, See Sacred Band of Thebes
toevah, 95-96, 99-100
trans/transgender, 12, 15, 29-31, 57, 73, 78, 128, 137-138, 162, 168
    self-harm/suicide among, 56-59, 162
Tushnet, Eve, 155-157

United Methodist Church, 134, 159
unmarried persons, See single life

Vines, Matthew, 10, 11, 45, 47-48, 53-54, 57, 59, 89-90, 92-93, 95, 99, 122, 124-125, 128, 162
virgin/virginity, 62, 73

Zeus, 112

ACKNOWLEDGEMENTS

I must thank a long list of teachers, friends, and persons who hold contradictory positions to the one I have laid out in this book for their contributions to it. Perhaps it is the third group to whom I owe the most. I have read more of their work than the writings of people who share my view. Why? I try to be fair. I want to know if I have overlooked something. I am not so arrogant as to believe that others may not be in possession of facts I have missed or can make arguments I have not considered. This "long list" is far too long for me to begin a litany of names.

In terms of specific persons, however, I must thank my wife for insisting that I write *The Ink Is Dry*. Myra was always my proofreader and first editor on everything from several years of newspaper columns to the final volume we produced together. *Male and Female God Created Them* is a 400+ page resource book for people who want to dig into the historical, cultural, linguistic, and textual arguments on same-sex relationships. As we moved to its completion and although she saw it only in its pre-publication form before her death, she insisted, "Okay, I understand the need for this 'big book' with all those footnotes. Now you need to write one for people like me."

Although she was smarter than me on practically everything, she didn't have the interest or background I had pursued in history, philosophy, languages, and theology that tends to write things "with all those footnotes." Because she believed the subject matter is important and that the unprecedented availability of misinformation about it has led some very good people to draw some very bad conclusions, she wanted a version written on a popular level. Or, as she put it, she believed a shorter book with fewer detailed arguments was more likely to be read by the average person than the big book. I agree. And I promised her this book would be written as soon as possible. Grief over her death slowed the work significantly, but a promise is a promise.

I thank Doug Peters and Jason Thompson for reminding me to stay about the fulfillment of my promise. More than that, I thank them for their patience and loving support through the most difficult time of my life. With space, I could also name specific moments of encouragement from the persons whose endorsements of the book appear on its first few pages.

I thank Karl Halverson at College Press for his enthusiastic reception of *Male and Female God Created Them* and his decision to get it printed and distributed as a resource volume for academics, preachers, and teachers. He has continued to support the production of *The Ink Is Dry* in spite of and through a recent surgery and recovery from it.

I thank Angela Blethen, also at College Press, for her day-to-day proficiency in the logistics of getting my manuscript into the form that is in your hands now. Accommodating, cheerful, and professional at every step along the way, she has been wonderful to keep the project moving – even as she and her husband await the birth of their first child.

Above all, I thank the gracious God who called me to his service decades ago. Insufficient as I am and have been, thank you, Holy Father, Blessed Son, and Indwelling Spirit, for the grace of that call and for blessing my meager offerings to your purposes and occasional glory.

Finally, thank *you* – reader of this book – for the time you may choose to spend with it in your search to clarify and live God's will for your life. I pray for our Father to bless us both as we grow in love for him and fidelity to his will.

www.ingramcontent.com/pod-product-compliance
Lightning Source LLC
Chambersburg PA
CBHW070149100426
42743CB00013B/2861